A D V

"Danny Kofke has created a must-read for all educators. Whether just starting in the profession or a veteran, *The Wealthy Teacher* is chock full of information about doing what needs to be done to be able to live comfortably on a teacher's income, as well as developing the nest egg to retire. His format makes the information memorable and easy to understand. Danny's explanation of insurance is perfect! *The Wealthy Teacher* should be required reading for all teachers!"

DR. STEVEN MILETTO, 2009 Georgia Principal of the Year, Finalist for 2010 National Principal of the Year, Executive Director Heart of Georgia, RESA

"*The Wealthy Teacher* is the perfect blueprint for financial success no matter what your salary. Danny Kofke's advice is spot on whether you want to save more money, reduce debt or better plan for retirement. You'll also love his many surprising insights – like how to fully own your home in just seven years, and why teachers are actually better investors than almost any other profession. I highly recommend this book!"

LYNNETTE KHALFANI-COX, The Money Coach, author of the *New York Times* bestseller *Zero Debt*

THE
Wealthy
Teacher

❦ THE ❦
Wealthy
Teacher

Lessons for Prospering on a
School Teacher's Salary

D A N N Y   K O F K E

Wyatt-MacKenzie Publishing
DEADWOOD, OREGON

The Wealthy Teacher
Lessons for Prospering on a School Teacher's Salary
Danny Kofke

ISBN: 978-1-942545-94-1
Library of Congress Control Number: 2017956610

"What the Rich Do Every Day" by Tom Corley used with permission.

"Poll Results: Teachers" used with permission from YouGov.

The publisher and editors do not assume any legal responsibility for errors,
omissions or claims, nor do they provide any warranty, expressed or implied,
with respect to information published. Although the author has made every
effort to ensure that the information in this book was correct at press time,
the author and publisher do not assume and hereby disclaim any liability to
any party for any loss, damage, or disruption caused by errors or omissions,
whether such errors or omissions result from negligence, accident, or any
other cause.

Wyatt-MacKenzie Publishing
DEADWOOD, OREGON

Wyatt-MacKenzie Publishing, Inc.
www.WyattMacKenzie.com
Contact us: info@wyattmackenzie.com

Dedicated to all you teachers out there.
Thank you for making this world a better place.

TABLE OF CONTENTS

How I Thrived on My Teacher's Salary

I knew I wanted to be a teacher after having Mr. Stutzke in 9th grade. He taught Civics and was just one of those special teachers who many of us have had (if you are a teacher reading this, you probably had that special teacher who led you into the profession). Mr. Stutzke was that teacher for me. Even though I was in his class over 25 years ago, I still remember his motto: "Stand and Deliver." Anytime a student had something to say, she had to stand by her desk and say it. Looking back now, I had no clue how this would help prepare me for my future. Like most teenagers, I was nervous to get up in front of the room and speak to the class. This practice that Mr. Stutzke employed forced us to speak in front of the class in a less threatening way. As an adult, I have presented in rooms full of hundreds of people and I am not ever nervous. I have Mr. Stutzke to thank for helping me with this!

A Change in Plans

In addition to wanting to be a teacher, I also wanted to coach high school baseball (I played in high school and at a junior college). After graduation, I planned on majoring in history to become a high school history teacher and coach.

However, after obtaining my Associate Arts degree from a local community college, I took a semester off. During this time, I got a job at a preschool and taught a class of 3-year-olds. I had no clue this experience would change my career path. I absolutely LOVED the little ones and felt a great responsibility towards them. There were some who had no fathers in their lives and I was their only positive male influence. Pretty powerful.

I then thought about my initial career choice. If I were to continue with my major and graduated with a history degree, my options would be somewhat limited. There are only a set number of history teachers in a school district. Because I enjoyed teaching young children, I decided to change my major to elementary education. This degree would enable me to teach grades K-6. Most districts have numerous elementary schools, so I would have a much better chance of getting a job out of college.

Love at First Sight

After taking that semester off, I went back to school with my new major and was finished with my coursework a year and a half later. I was then assigned to student teach in a first-grade classroom.

I showed up in Mrs. Cindy Rodriguez's classroom on the first teacher workday in 1999 and immediately fell for another first-grade teacher: Tracy. She was a natural-born teacher and just amazing. It was a crazy courtship and we were engaged in December of that year, married the following June, and were living and teaching in another country on the one-year anniversary of the day we met! Having two daughters of my own now, I can clearly see why her parents were a little worried that she was rushing into this marriage; however, 17 years later, we are still going strong.

Our European Adventure

Shortly before getting engaged (we had already picked out the ring so we knew we were going to get married), Tracy and I looked into possibly teaching abroad. We had a teacher friend who knew other educators who taught overseas and they absolutely loved it. Now at this point in my life I really knew nothing about other countries and could not even locate many on a map. However, it sounded like a promising opportunity so Tracy and I started researching to see if this was something we wanted to pursue

Our first step was to find out how we could even apply to teach at a school located in another country. We discovered that we could go through a company called International Schools Services (ISS). We discovered a potential roadblock: ISS was looking for teachers that possessed a bachelor's degree and had at least two years of full-time teaching experience under their belts. At this point in time, I had not graduated college yet, so had no teaching experience in the public school setting. There was a special clause we noticed that helped us get in, however; ISS encouraged teaching teams to apply. If a school was able to fill two spots at once, it was a great benefit to them. In addition, because we would be living together, the school would only have to find one place for us to live rather than two if we were applying as individuals. So, I rode Tracy's coattails and we applied as a team.

We had to each pay a fee (at that time it was $175/person) and complete two narratives. The first asked us to write a statement describing the personal and professional qualifications and experiences we had that would enable us to be successful in an international school. The second asked us to tell what made us outstanding educators. We completed these, sent in our money, and then waited to hear back.

After what seemed like forever (but was really only a month), we received word in late December that we had been accepted. We then made plans to attend a hiring fair that ISS had scheduled in mid-February in Boston.

To say we were overwhelmed upon arriving at that job fair is an understatement. There were schools from over 200 countries represented there! Schools located in countries and places I didn't even know existed were represented. We were very fortunate that a few directors (principals) had read our resumes and wanted to interview us. Tracy and I interviewed with schools that were located in Bahrain, Nigeria, and Poland.

The school in Bahrain offered us a job right after our interview. We asked if we could have an hour to discuss it. We went with our gut feelings and decided to turn them down. This was somewhat risky because attending this hiring fair had cost us about $1,000 when all was said and done and we were not guaranteed anything from it. We had to risk leaving Boston without any other offers, but had to decide according to what felt right.

We then interviewed with the school in Nigeria and it went well. Our last interview was for a school in Krakow, Poland. After this, we walked around Boston for a little while trying to decompress. This was a very crazy and hectic day and we needed some fresh air.

After a somewhat restless night, we received a call in the morning from Melissa, the director of the school in

Krakow, telling us we had a follow-up interview with her in one hour. At least we had someone else interested in us! We felt this interview went well and Melissa said she would be in touch the following day before we left Boston. Now the waiting game was on.

The next day we sat around our hotel room waiting for that call. As you can imagine, after a few hours, we were starting to lose our minds. Tracy and I decided to explore Boston some more and figured we would have a message when we got back to the hotel. Right we were; upon returning there was a message from Melissa saying, "Have a safe trip home. I will call you there." AAHHH!! We flew home that night with our lives still on hold.

Melissa finally called the next morning and told us that the American International School of Krakow was offering Tracy and me each a job. I would be teaching a kindergarten/first-grade class and Tracy a second/third/fourth-grade class. We were unaware at the time, but this experience would not only lead to some great adventures, but also set the foundation for our financial success (more on this in a bit).

Moving Home

Tracy and I had signed a two-year contract to teach in Poland. We debated about staying longer but wanted to have children. Both of our families lived in the same town (Vero Beach, Florida) so we decided that two years was long enough, after which we moved back home. We both got jobs teaching first grade and the next chapter began.

Shortly after moving home, we discussed when we wanted to have children and what life would look like after that event. Now, ultimately it is up to *Him* if and when this will happen, but we did have a small say in the matter. We decided it would be best for Tracy to be able to take off at least one year after having a baby, so we came up with the plan for us to start trying after we were home for a year. This would allow us time to build up our savings and pay off as much debt as possible so we could live off my teacher's salary alone, about $37,000 a year at that time. In fact, looking back, we actually planned for this moment upon arriving in Poland!

Planning Ahead

Tracy and I left Florida in August of 2000 to embark on teaching in Poland. This was probably the most difficult thing either of us had ever done in our lives up to that point. We were leaving the friendly confines of our homes in The States and going to a place where we didn't even speak the language! But hey, what doesn't kill you makes you stronger. The first few weeks there it was a challenge to even buy a bottle of water; but, after a month, we got used to our "new" lives and it became easier.

There were many wonderful things about living in Poland. The class sizes were much smaller than in The States, the students were all very well-behaved, we had the chance to travel a lot, and at the same time, had an opportunity to save some money. Our salaries were close to what a teaching salary was in Florida with one exception: we did not have to pay taxes. During the years we taught in Krakow, Americans were allowed to earn up to $75,000 a year overseas without having to pay taxes on it. In addition, the school paid for our utilities and housing so we didn't have many expenses. The public transportation system was wonderful so we went without a car for those two years. Because we knew we wanted to return home after this adventure with money in the bank, we decided to use all of these accommodations to our advantage and plan ahead.

Shortly before leaving for Krakow, Tracy and I discussed how much money we would like to have in savings when we returned home. This was the first important financial decision we made as a couple. Many people spend all their income and then some. To combat this, we decided to pay ourselves first before we could become accustomed to spending our entire income.

We figured that $20,000 would be a good amount to have in the bank upon arriving home after teaching in Poland. Since we signed a two-year contract, we went with the assumption that we would be there for two years. So, we divided $20,000 by 24 months (2 years) and came up with $834 per month. Once we arrived in Krakow, we made plans with the secretary of the school to automatically deposit this amount into our savings account each monthly pay period, and had the rest deposited into our checking account for us to live off of. By doing this from the beginning, we never missed this money because we never got used to it being part of our income.

A Two-Year Honeymoon

The greatest part about paying ourselves first was knowing that we could spend the entire amount in our checking account without feeling any guilt because we were automatically saving a good amount each month for our eventual return back home. As this was a once-in-a-lifetime opportunity, Tracy and I wanted to take full advantage of it and travel as much as possible.

In October, we spent a long weekend in Prague, Czech Republic. In November, we went off for a 5-day trip to Nice, France. While there, we wined and dined with the wealthy in Monte Carlo. We decided to fly home in December to spend Christmas with our families.

The year 2001 saw us in many places. In February we visited Tunisia, Africa for a week. Spring break in April was spent in Florence and Venice, Italy (we even rode in a gondola in Venice and considered this our belated honeymoon). To kick off our summer, we spent one week in Seville, Spain and then met my family for a week of fun in Costa del Sol. My grandparents, parents, and brother then flew back to Krakow with us and spent a week there exploring our new home. We went back to Prague in September during a long weekend. October saw us in Paris, France during our fall break. At the beginning of November, we visited Berlin, Germany. The week before Thanksgiving, we went to The Hague, Netherlands. We decided to stay in Europe for the holidays and spent Christmas week in Vienna, Austria. Not your average year, huh?

By January 2002, we knew we would be heading home in June so we decided to continue traveling as much as possible. In January, we took a school field trip to the mountainous Polish city of Zakopane for skiing and sled rides. We spent our winter break in Budapest, Hungary. Tracy's mom and grandmother came over to visit during our spring break and we headed back to Vienna with them for a few days.

We headed home in June having visited a grand total of 11 countries! In addition, we had $20,000 in the bank to start our lives. This was all possible because we made a plan and stuck to it.

The Planning Continues

We had already decided that we wanted Tracy to be able to stay home when we had a child. In order to accomplish this goal, we had to be very mindful of how we spent money and of the decisions we made.

Our first major choice was buying a car. We had planned

on using some of our savings to put a down payment on two cars, one for each of us. I mean, everyone has to have a car, right? Well, living for two years without having even one car made us rethink this. What if we could get by on only one automobile? That would help us achieve our goal of having Tracy being able to stay home. We decided to give it a whirl and just purchased one car for us to share.

Sharing a car was not always easy. We were hired to teach at two different schools. The plan most of the time was for me to drop Tracy off at her school and then drive to mine. This was not too difficult, because our schools were within a 5-mile radius of our house. However, there were occasional days that Tracy had a meeting at another location after school and needed the car. What to do then? On those occasions, as we lived only about two miles from my school, I rode my bike to work. Yes, you read that correctly. I was the only teacher who parked his bike at the bike rack. There were some who made fun of me for this. I heard comments such as, "Get off your wallet, Danny."

This is when I learned another valuable lesson. If people who have no money are making fun of you, keep doing what you are doing! I know this is much easier said than done, but it is so true. I mean, if I went to a personal trainer and he weighed 400 pounds I would do the complete opposite of what he told me to do unless I wanted to look like him. Why let broke people dictate how you spend money unless you want to end up like them: broke?

Because we only had one car, we added extra each month to our payment (we pretended like we had two car payments and paid this entire amount towards our one car), which enabled us to pay it off in two years. I am proud to write that I still drive that same car we bought over 15 years ago and haven't had a car payment on it for over 13 years!

Another major decision we had to make was buying a

house. The conventional wisdom at this time was to get qual-
ified for as much as you could and then buy as much house
as your lender said you could afford. However, this strategy
would work against our goal of having Tracy being able to
stay home. We shopped around a bit and found a beautiful
two-bedroom home that was way below the amount for
which we could qualify. We quickly signed the dotted line,
and within two months of moving home, had a car and a
house. Our American Dream had begun.

The Planning Pays-Off

Over the next two years, Tracy and I continued to follow
the plan we had made. On May 26th, 2004, we were blessed
to have Ava. Shortly after she was born, the car was paid off.
This would enable us to have Tracy stay home with her.

We then changed plans a little bit. There is a law that
was passed in 1993 titled the Family and Medical Leave Act.
This law allows up to 12 weeks of job-protected, unpaid leave
when you have a child. We decided that I would stay home
for two months at the beginning of the following school
year with Ava and then Tracy would stay home the rest of
the year. This helped us save money on our health insurance
and gave me valuable time with Ava.

Changes in Latitudes, Changes in Attitudes

Things were drumming along smoothly and we were
getting used to having a baby in our lives. In September of
2004, something happened that caused us to rethink our
long-term plans. In a span of 24 days, we were hit with 2
hurricanes! The second one left behind a lot of damage and
we needed a new roof, new carpet, and a new back porch.
This got us thinking a bit. We had always wanted to live in a

location where the weather wasn't always so hot. I know some people love the hot weather but having spent many a Christmas wearing shorts and a t-shirt, this just wasn't for us. After these hurricanes, we entertained the thought of moving out of Florida; however, after some thought, we decided against it since we were starting to settle in.

A big change happened towards the end of the 2004-05 school year. I was very happy and content teaching first grade but was offered a job selling high-end flooring. There was the potential for me to double and even triple my teaching salary. It was a difficult decision because I loved being a teacher, but we decided I should give it a whirl since this larger salary would enable Tracy to stay home even longer. So, my last day of teaching was in June and I started selling flooring in August. In addition, Tracy got back into teaching but not full time. She decided to team teach with another teacher and taught three days a week. On the days that Tracy taught, Ava went to my parents' one day, my grandparents' another and a good family friend the third day. This enabled us to bring in a little more income while I made a career transition.

This schedule was going well and then October came. We had all of our Halloween decorations up and, a week before this holiday, they had to come down because a hurricane was on the way. This one was not as powerful as the two that hit the previous year but we still lost our power for a week. While this seemed horrible at the time, it was really a blessing in disguise. This prompted Tracy and I to discuss the possibility of moving again. We never really liked the South Florida weather and dealing with hurricanes was the straw that broke the camel's back. We decided to put our house up for sale and move to North Georgia.

Georgia On My Mind

My entire family vacationed in the north Georgia mountains during the summer of 2005 and really enjoyed it. That was pretty much all we knew about Georgia but decided that was where we wanted to move. Tracy, my parents, and grandmother took a 4-day trip to look around north Georgia in early 2006. They drove around and Tracy found a few houses that she liked. We planned on returning to search together in March, during her spring break.

Something completely unexpected happened shortly before we headed to Georgia the next time. I was not really satisfied in my new job. I had gone from teaching first grade, watching my students experience growth and learn how to read and write, to selling area rugs that cost over $5,000. The sad part was that I didn't really care if someone bought expensive flooring and, thus, was a horrible salesperson in that area. I guess coming from something as important as teaching to doing sales wasn't as easy as I thought it would be. I discovered that the potential to make more money wasn't worth it; I am a teacher at heart. Around that time, there happened to be an opening at Tracy's school, teaching autistic students. I interviewed for this position and was hired. So, a little after nine months of teaching what I thought might be my last class, I was happily back in!

Tracy, Ava, and I visited Georgia in March and found a house we liked. Our house in Florida had sold shortly after being put on the market so all that was left was for us to finish out the school year. We came back in May and closed on our new house in Georgia. I also went to a local school that had an opening teaching special needs students and was hired. So we now had a house and a job waiting for us in Georgia! In addition, my parents and grandparents were both ready for a change, too, and decided to move from

Florida to our new town in Georgia. It was all coming together.

Staying Home Longer

We were fortunate that this move came when the housing market was strong. We made a good profit from selling our house in Florida and were able to put down a good amount on our house in Georgia. This made our monthly mortgage payments very manageable on my teaching salary; therefore, Tracy would be able to stay home indefinitely, which had been our big goal all along!

In 2007, we added another daughter, Ella, to our family. I was earning around $42,000 a year teaching, and we were able to comfortably live off that. Now granted, we didn't drive fancy cars or dine at expensive restaurants, but we had the freedom to pursue our desires: me to teach and Tracy to stay home and raise Ava and Ella. Through sound planning and living below our means, Tracy was able to stay home full time a total of eight years. In addition, despite living off my teacher's salary alone during this time, we have no debt except our mortgage (which, as I write this, is scheduled to be paid off in less than one year), are on track to retire with a sizable nest egg, have a one-year emergency fund in place, and most important, live wealthy lives on less. The great thing about it is, if we can do it, you can, too.

Back Into the Classroom

We were managing on my salary alone, but started looking ahead. At some point we would both need new cars, our house would start needing repairs, and the kids would want to participate in activities. At that point, both Ava and Ella had started elementary school, so Tracy had been able to stay home with both of them until they entered school: our main goal.

Around this time, there happened to be a second grade teaching position open at the school were I taught and the girls attended; how perfect was that? Tracy interviewed and was hired. We decided to take this year-by-year to see how much of an impact it would have on our family. Our main goal was to sock away as much as possible in our savings account so that Tracy could stay home again when the time was right.

More Isn't Always Better

Even though we had more than doubled our income, an interesting thing happened: we were not happier. In fact, I would say we were much more stressed out! You all know firsthand how difficult teaching is. After stepping out of the classroom for a few years (more on that in a minute), I have new appreciation for how hard teaching is. In fact, after teaching second grade for three years, Tracy became a technology coach at her school and currently works part-time (she alternates between working three days one week and two days the next). She would come home after teaching second grade and be completely exhausted. She felt she was not giving Ava and Ella all she could because she was so drained. Even though we live off less again, our lives are much wealthier!

This would not have been possible if we had not planned ahead. It would have been very easy to live up to our new income, but we chose to pay ourselves first and set a good amount aside so that we would have options. I know that some equate wealth with material things but I think of being wealthy as being able to choose what you want to do. When Tracy (and *He*) decided it was time for a change, we were able to make this change because of how we view wealth.

Becoming an Author

Some of my colleagues noticed how Tracy and I lived differently from many. Shortly before Ava was born, some even suggested that I write a book telling how we did this. I didn't really give this much thought until one November weekend in 2005. Tracy (and Ava) had gone to visit her sister and I was home alone. I think *He* put an image in my head to sit down and start writing. As I look back on this time, that is the only explanation I have. I listened and some amazing things have happened.

I continued to write, and after a few months, had my words on paper. I really had no intention of really doing anything with this. I just thought it was neat to have my thoughts down to share with my family and some friends. One of them suggested I try to publish it. I did some research and submitted it to a few publishers. One of them accepted it with a clause: I would have to pony up almost $4,000 to have it published! Tracy and I discussed and prayed about this and decided it was worth the risk. In October of 2007, *How To Survive (and perhaps thrive) On A Teacher's Salary* was released.

This book was the start of an amazing ride. Fast-forward 10 years since I started writing it and my life has drastically changed because of this book. I have written two other books: *A Bright Financial Future: Teaching Kids About Money Pre-K through College for Life-Long Success* and *A Simple Book of Financial Wisdom: Teach Yourself (and Your Kids) How to Live Wealthy with Little Money.* In addition, Ava (who is now 13) traditionally published her own book in September 2014 titled *The Financial Angel: What All Kids Should Know About Money.*

These books have led me to be interviewed on television more than 50 times and counting. Some were national shows such as *The CBS Early Show, Fox & Friends, CNN's Newsroom,* Fox

Business Network's *The Willis Report*, HLN's *Weekend Express*, *The 700 Club*, *The Clark Howard Show*, and *MSNBC Live*. I have also been interviewed on over 600 radio shows and featured in numerous publications such as *USA Today*, *Consumer Reports*, *Yahoo.com*, *Money Magazine*, *Bankrate.com*, *Instructor Magazine*, *The Atlanta Journal Constitution*, *Woman's Day*, and *The Wall Street Journal*. Being an author led me to a job in which I got to travel throughout Georgia and help other teachers save money. In addition, numerous doors have opened (and others will open) because of these books.

Let's Go

Okay, now you know my story and it is time for you to change yours. In the pages that follow, I will lay out the plan that has enabled my family to live wealthy on a moderate teacher's salary. Teachers are some of the most gracious people I have met. You all give so much of yourselves and I want to help give back to you. I hear the bell ringing; class is in session.

CHAPTER 1

Why Are We Broke?

"Too many people spend money they haven't earned,
to buy things they don't want, to impress
people they don't like."
WILL ROGERS

Before we jump into the ways you can win with money,
let's take a look at some pretty sobering statistics. According
to Bankrate's Financial Security Index poll:

- 24 percent of Americans have no emergency
  savings at all

- Another 20 percent said their emergency savings
  would cover, at best, three months' worth of
  expenses

- Only three out of ten said they have six months'
  worth of expenses for use in emergency, the minimum recommended by many financial planning
  experts.[a]

So, according to this poll, a minority of Americans have an adequate amount of money saved to cover unexpected emergencies and/or opportunities. YIKES!

It is very difficult to get ahead financially when you owe others money and have nothing saved.

I know you are in a profession that doesn't pay that great but let's take a look at your salary compared to the world at large. By global standards:

- If you make $37,000 a year you are in the top 4 percent of wage earners

- If you make $50,000 or more a year you are in the top 1 percent [b]

In fact, if you live in America, you have a much richer life than almost anyone else living in another country. The problem is that we tend to focus on our circle of friends and compare what we don't have to what they do have. We think it is a tragedy when we can't get a signal on our cell phone, yet thousands of people will go to sleep hungry tonight. Looking at the bigger picture can help us greatly.

Unfortunately, we usually compare ourselves to our current situation rather than looking at the bigger picture. I know how much we make and how "rich" we feel is based on our own personal perspective. However, by taking a look at the numbers, I hope we realize that most people have it so much better than countless others. In fact, most of us don't have an income problem: we have an outgo one.

Good News For Teachers

While teachers are vastly underpaid (I know I am preaching to the choir here and there will be more on that in a bit)

I have some great news for you. Despite not getting paid a large salary, teachers are actually better investors than almost any other profession!

Openfolio, an online platform where investors privately and publicly share their investment holdings, analyzed 20,000 investors. According to this analysis, school teachers averaged better returns on their investments than people from any other profession.[c] So why were teachers so successful? Openfolio found two common characteristics among teachers:

1) Teachers were more patient than other investors.

2) Teachers were more likely than others to diversify their investments. Rather than just put all their eggs in one basket, teachers had their money spread out over numerous investment options.

We cover retirement later on, but this is great news for you going forward: statistically, you are part of a profession that does very well with their investments.

Despite this, some of us still find ourselves with little or nothing to invest. So what are some of the reasons we get into trouble with money? Let's take a look.

Reasons We Get Into Trouble With Money

1. Lack of Contentment

Many of us are rich but we don't feel like it. We look at others and wish we had what they had. Here are some truths about losing contentment:

- The more we shop, the more we spend.
- The more we watch television, the more we spend.
- The more time we spend looking through catalogs, the more we spend.
- The more we read magazine ads, the more we spend.

- The more time we spend surfing the web, the more we spend.

I know these seem pretty obvious but many of us don't give these truths much thought. Madison Avenue spends billions of dollars every year to entice us to part with our money, but how hard they try really hit home for me recently. I was watching The World Series and a Christmas commercial came on. It was not even Halloween yet! In fact, some digital marketing experts estimate that most Americans are exposed to between 4,000 and 10,000 advertisements each day. [d]

To illustrate the power of ads a little more, read the following story:

A large manufacturing firm decided to open a new assembly plant in an underdeveloped Latin American country because labor was cheap and plentiful. The plant was successfully opened and the operation was progressing smoothly, until the first paycheck. The next day, none of the villagers reported for work. Management waited ... one, two, three days. Still no villagers came to work. The plant manager went to see the village chief to find out the problem. "Why should we continue to work?" the chief asked in response to the manager's inquiry. "We are satisfied. We have already earned all the money we need to live on." The plant stood idle for almost a month. Then someone came up with the idea of distributing Sears catalogs to all the villagers. Reading the catalogs created new needs in the lives of the villagers. Since that time, there has not been an unemployment problem.

I can definitely relate to that story. Sometimes ignorance can be bliss. Try to find contentment in what you have and you won't feel like you are lacking in anything. A great saying to help with this is, "Want what you have and you will always have what you want." Makes perfect sense on paper, but then we are bombarded by advertisements and our emotions kick in and we want what others have, not just what we already have. Once we realize we could have more, many of us automatically want more. The key is to try to find a level of contentment so that you do not have to compare yourself to others and to how much more "stuff" they have than you do.

Be Content With What You Have

Before we take a look at ways to get out of debt, we need to keep this mentality in mind. I realize feeling content and happy with what we have is totally based on our current perspective, but sometimes we need to step outside our small boxes and what is currently going on in our lives to realize how blessed we truly are. Take some time and make a list of everything for which you are grateful. Grab a piece of paper right now, and make a list of 20!

I also encourage you to challenge each member of your family to list the things they are grateful for, too. For some of you, there is not enough room to list everything you are grateful for whereas for others, you might not be able to think of more than ten right now. That is ok. Just refer back to this page often (I encourage you to do so at least one time every day for at least one month) and I bet many ideas will come pouring in.

An Attitude of Gratitude

I know it can be easy to get caught in all the things we have to accomplish in a day, but something that really helps me start my day right is quiet time with God, thanking Him for all that He has given me. I sit on my front porch in the wee morning hours when the weather allows it (yes, it does get cold here in north Georgia) and start my day off with prayer and gratitude. Not too long ago, I looked up at a beautiful and clear sky. As I looked up at all the stars, I thanked Him for making them. As if in on cue, I saw a shooting star. It gave me chills. He was saying, "You're welcome." If that doesn't get you fired up first thing in the morning, I don't know what will!

Something else that changed the way I look at life was teaching special needs children. I taught what is known in Georgia as a self-contained Severe/Profound Class. The students had severe and profound mental and physical disabilities and their IQs were under 30. I had some in wheelchairs, some that had to be tube-fed, most needed assistance with toileting and all had communication needs. However, despite these limitations, most of them were extremely happy. I felt pretty silly complaining about my situation when I was able to do much more than they were. Some used to say that those students were lucky to have me as their teacher, but I know the opposite is true. I was the lucky one and the lessons they taught me will last a lifetime!

2. We Don't Have Goals or a Plan

Another reason people don't handle money well is that they have not set goals and, thus, do not have a plan. Benjamin Franklin said, "If you fail to plan, you are planning to fail." This is why almost one-fourth of us have nothing saved.

If you don't have a destination in mind, it is hard to get there.

I am directionally challenged. If I were to dive from Georgia to Florida, I would need a GPS device to help me get there. Without it, I might end up in North Carolina! Using a GPS device enables me to see checkpoints along the way to ensure I am heading in the correct direction. The same holds true with saving money: we first need a plan. Let's say your goal is to have $6,000 in your savings account this time next year. Now we have a goal and can work on achieving it. We divide $6,000 by 12 months to establish a monthly goal. We can easily keep track of this monthly goal. We now know what we need to save each month to ensure we achieve the goal. We must then come up with a plan of attack to save $500 each month.

We first came up with a goal. Then we looked at a way to track progress. Finally, we came up with a plan that would help us achieve this goal. Without having these checkpoints in place, it would be very difficult to save money because we would not clearly see our progress.

3. We Try to Keep up With the Wrong People

A final reason many people are broke is that they try to emulate others. I know some who even try to impress people they don't know! They buy really expensive cars they truly cannot afford to impress someone next to them at a red light. They may get a look of jealousy from that person, but will probably never even see them again. Trying to impress others is a recipe for disaster.

Warren Buffett is a perfect example of someone who doesn't try to keep up with others nor cares about what they think about him. He is ranked among the richest people in the world, yet he lives the same way he lived before he had billions of dollars. He still resides in the same house he bought in 1958 for $31,500. He is also known for his simple tastes like McDonald's hamburgers and Cherry Coke.

Mr. Buffett often says, "The first rule of investing is don't lose money; the second rule is don't forget Rule No. 1." This carries over into his personal life as well. Despite having a net worth over $60 billion, he earns a base salary of $100,000 a year from Berkshire Hathaway. Since he has simple tastes, he is able to easily live off this salary.

In an interview, Mr. Buffett described success as this: "Success is really doing what you love and doing it well. It's as simple as that. Really getting to do what you love to do every day—that's really the ultimate luxury ... your standard of living is not equal to your cost of living."[e]

WOW. He hit the nail on the head. I did not get into teaching to make a lot of money. I got into teaching because I had a passion for helping others. Over time, this passion prompted me to write books. I now get to use my teaching skills and help others with their finances. Some days are more difficult than others and it is not all rainbows and butterflies, but I am doing exactly what I feel called to do. That is definitely something that you cannot put a price tag on.

Mr. Buffett is happy with what he has. He is not interested in a bigger house or a newer car. He really could care less about what his neighbors have. The thing is, unless you are the wealthiest person on earth, there will always be someone with more. If you are continuously looking to live up to others, you will find yourself broke. It doesn't matter how much you have coming in; if you spend more than you earn, you won't have any money. This holds true whether you make $10,000, $100,000, or even $1,000,000 a year.

To further illustrate this, what do 50 Cent, Marvin Gaye, Don Johnson, and our current President all have in common? Even though they all made a lot of money, they all ended up making unwise choices with it.[f, g, h, i]

They may have lost contentment, didn't have a plan, or tried to keep up with others (or maybe all three), and as a result found themselves out of money. Try at all costs to avoid those three things, and you will position yourself to win with money.

Money Issues Mostly Result From
Behavior, Not Math

Most of us can figure out how much interest we will be paying if we get into debt; it is basic eighth-grade math. Yet, millions still do. Why is this? Obviously it is not the math! For most of us, money problems center around our behavior.

On his website RichHabitsInstitute.com, Tom Corley outlines a few of the differences between the habits of the rich and the poor. I found this list very interesting and wanted to share it with you:

What the Rich Do Every Day

1. 70% of wealthy eat less than 300 junk food calories per day. 97% of poor people eat more than 300 junk food calories per day. 23% of wealthy gamble. 52% of poor people gamble.

2. 80% of wealthy are focused on accomplishing some single goal. Only 12% of the poor do this.

3. 76% of wealthy exercise aerobically four days a week. 23% of poor do this.

4. 63% of wealthy listen to audio books during commute to work versus 5% of poor people.

5. 81% of wealthy maintain a to-do list versus 19% of poor.

6. 63% of wealthy parents make their children read two or more non-fiction books a month versus 3% of poor.

7. 70% of wealthy parents make their children volunteer 10 hours or more a month versus 3% of poor.

8. 80% of wealthy make Happy Birthday calls versus 11% of poor.

9. 67% of wealthy write down their goals versus 17% of poor.

10. 88% of wealthy read 30 minutes or more each day for education or career reasons versus 2% of poor.

11. 6% of wealthy say what's on their mind versus 69% of poor.

12. 79% of wealthy network five hours or more each month versus 16% of poor.

13. 67% of wealthy watch one hour or less of TV every day versus 23% of poor.

14. 6% of wealthy watch reality TV versus 78% of poor.

15. 44% of wealthy wake up three hours before work starts versus 3% of poor.

16. 74% of wealthy teach good daily success habits to their children versus 1% of poor.

17. 84% of wealthy believe good habits create opportunity luck versus 4% of poor.

18. 76% of wealthy believe bad habits create detrimental luck versus 9% of poor.

19. 86% of wealthy believe in lifelong educational self-improvement versus 5% of poor.

20. 86% of wealthy love to read versus 26% of poor.[j]

I know that not all of these are money related but I found it very interesting that all of these good and poor outcomes were based on our behavior. I find that to be a positive thing. You see, gaining control of your finances is not hard on paper; it is your behavior that has much more to do with controlling your finances than anything else. In the pages to come I will give you a plan to follow so that the guesswork is removed. You can do this!

YOUR HOMEWORK

Take a moment and think: are you spending money because you are trying to mask some sort of unhappiness you have? If so, think about ways you can become more content without having to spend money.

Establish some financial goals. After you have these goals, develop a plan to achieve these.

Are you trying to keep up with some of your friends or others?

CHAPTER 2

Does Money Make Us Happy?

"Teachers affect eternity; no one can tell
where their influence stops."
HENRY BROOKS ADAMS

Like we discussed before, if more goes out than comes in, you will eventually find yourself with no money. If you make $100,000 but spend $100,100 this principle still applies.

I know it sounds pretty basic and, on paper, it is. So why do so many of us find ourselves in debt? I feel this goes back to contentment. As Americans, we live in one of the richest nations on Earth. Despite that, many of us are unhappy. In fact, according to a recent study, almost 70 percent of Americans are miserable with their jobs.[a]

Is it any wonder then that so many spend money they truly should not be spending or even have? When you spend most of your waking hours at a place you don't like, it is very tempting to reward yourself for this by purchasing material things. However, the feeling you get with this new item goes away quickly. Then you are in a vicious cycle of having to buy stuff to bring about a false sense of happiness. Think about it, we live in a country that a offers a "new car" fragrance so that we can pretend that we are driving a brand new car (on the flip-side, that actually might be a good idea if it prevents some from actually buying a new car). The key is to find happiness in what you are doing on a daily basis so you don't have to buy it, or even try to buy it.

Are Teachers Underappreciated?

I know, it's a loaded question: of course you are not appreciated enough! Don't just take it from me, as many others feel this way, too.

In fact, according to a recent HuffPost/YouGov poll, most Americans agree that public school teachers should get paid more money and be treated with more respect.[b]

This poll asked participants the following questions and the responses follow.

In general, how would you rate the public school teachers in your community?

Excellent	13 percent
Good	45 percent
Fair	23 percent
Poor	6 percent
Not sure	14 percent

How would you rate your children's school teachers (this was asked of those who are the parent or guardian of any children under the age of 18)?

Excellent	25 percent
Good	43 percent
Fair	5 percent

Poor	3 percent
Does not apply to me	2 percent
Not sure	1 percent

Do you think most public school teachers:

Are paid too much	8 percent
Paid the right amount	28 percent
Paid too little	52 percent
Not sure	11 percent

In your community, do you think public school teachers are:

Underappreciated	43 percent
Treated about right	36 percent
Given too much attention	5 percent
Not sure	15 percent

Nationally, do you think public school teachers are:

Underappreciated	52 percent
Treated about right	26 percent
Given too much attention	8 percent
Not sure	13 percent

I hope that makes you feel a little better. I know it is really hard to not focus on that one negative parent alone, or the constant feeling that you are not appreciated. This survey shows that a majority of Americans feel your pain and wish you had it better.

Are Teachers Paid Enough?

I know, two crazy questions in a row! Once again, of course you are not paid what you are worth.

In fact, according to a recent report by the Center for American Progress, teachers not only have low starting pay but are also unlikely to have major salary increases even after being in the classroom for a few years. This lack of growth in teacher salaries really stands out when compared to other countries. When looking at this, the U.S. is behind numerous countries including Japan, Austria, and even my former home, Poland.

Overall, there are only four states (Connecticut, Maryland, New Jersey, and New York) in which teachers can max out their salary schedule above $80,000 a year. This report states, "The bottom line is that mid- and late-career teachers are not earning what they deserve, nor are they able to gain the salaries that support a middle-class existence."[c]

Even Though Your Salary is Low,
Are Teachers Still Happy?

Even though many workers are not satisfied with their jobs, there has to be a salary that could help make them feel happy, right? Well, actually, there was a study conducted to find this out.[d]

Psychologist Daniel Kahneman and economist Angus Deaton evaluated 450,000 Americans to determine what that magic salary number is. It turns out that a yearly salary of $75,000 is the number after which people's day-to-day happiness no longer improves. I know most of you make way below that figure so I have some great news for some of you educators!

Even though I have never made anywhere near that magical salary, I am usually very happy and content in my job. I once heard that teaching is one of the most satisfying careers so I wanted to find out what other careers people felt happy in. I was in luck. Payscale recently conducted a survey to determine this. To compile its latest list, PayScale asked over two million professionals whether their work is meaningful and ranked almost 500 professions based on the percentage of people in each of those jobs who answered "yes."

There is a list of the top 13 most meaningful jobs in America along with their average median salary at http://www.businessinsider.com/most-meaningful-jobs-in-america-2015-7

Once you review the list, do you find it interesting that out of these 13 most meaningful careers, only four have a higher median salary than that magical $75,000 figure (with one of those four being barely above that amount)? I have to admit I was not too shocked. You see, all the careers in this list are a calling. While it would be nice to be a surgeon and make over $300K a year, I bet most of them choose this profession because they have a calling for it. I can't imagine the pressure they must face on a daily basis and money alone could not keep them coming back for more. I love that almost a quarter of these careers are in education. You all got into teaching to make a difference in this world. That is what fuels your fire, rather than your paycheck.

YOUR HOMEWORK

It is a given that you are underpaid. Make a list of the reasons you became a teacher in the first place and some of the successes you have experienced because you chose to make this world a better place.

CHAPTER 3

Getting Started
Stretch Your Teacher's Salary

*"Annual income twenty pounds, annual expenditure nineteen six,
result happiness.
Annual income twenty pounds, annual expenditure twenty pound
ought and six, result misery."*
CHARLES DICKENS

The Budget: What Is It?

To begin, we first need to know how our money is be-
having. This is where the budget comes into play. Now I
know many people despise the b-word just like they don't
like the d-word (diet). Both of these bring up negative emotions for many people because they associate the words with
being deprived of a desired item. I feel the opposite is true.
By creating a budget, you can actually have your money
work harder for you and, thus, eventually have more to
spend.

What exactly is a budget? In simple terms, it is a list of outgoing expenses compared with incoming money. It is a plan for how you are going to spend your hard-earned money. Some people get fancy and create elaborate spreadsheets to help them come up with a budget whereas others (like me) simply use a pen and paper to create one. No matter which route you take, a budget should help you easily see how much you have coming in and going out. It is a tool that will help you prioritize your spending so that you don't run out of money before the month comes to an end.

Why Should You Use One?

Now that you understand what a budget is and aren't so scared of that word anymore, we can discuss why you should use one.

First, keeping a detailed account of your income and outgo will help you identify those expenses that are not really necessary. Now it is pretty obvious that if you live in a house that is way above your means or drive a car that is too fancy for your salary, you will quickly find yourself in trouble. However, for many, it is those day-to-day expenses that add up quickly over time that lead to financial distress. For example, let's say you stop and get a coffee on the way to school each morning and then use the vending machine in the afternoon to purchase a snack and soft drink. You don't really feel this pain because the coffee only costs $2 and the afternoon drink and snack run $3. That's only $5 a day: not too bad. Well, that $5 a day over 190 days (the number of days most teachers work in a school year) adds up to almost $1,000! Think of what you could do with that $1,000 if you made your coffee at home and brought in snacks. I bet most of you could think of a nice summer vacation that you could use the money for instead.

Another reason you should use a budget is that it will make your money go farther. Looking at the above example, if you didn't keep a budget, you may not have even realized you were spending that much money on drinks and snacks. The budget enables you to see this and then eliminate these items from your spending habits. This helps stretch your paycheck and keeps more money in your account.

Finally, a budget encourages communication between spouses. This is so important because too many marriages are hanging on by a thread. Oftentimes, money issues become the final nail in the coffin. Starting a budget should be a team effort in which both spouses (and children, too) meet and participate in deciding what should be purchased and what the family's financial goals should be. A budget can be a great tool to help strengthen and maybe even save a marriage.

How Do We Get Started?

To determine your budget, you need to know how every dollar is either being spent or saved. To begin, we need to list our major expenses.

Your Major Expenses

Unfortunately, too many of us have no clue what our major expenses are or how much we spend on them. We just a write a check or pay our bills online without thinking twice about what this money is being used for. Let's start changing this.

Below is a list of the major expenses that many of us have. Please take the time to write down how much you spend on each of these items every month. If any of these don't apply to you, simply cross it off. If you have an expense that is not listed, add it to the list. Some of the items listed below might be a yearly payment for you (e.g., home owner's insurance, car insurance, etc.). If that is the case, divide your yearly figure by 12 to see how much you need to save each month to pay for these when they are due.

My Monthly Major Expenses

Savings
Retirement fund $ _____
College fund $ _____

Housing
Mortgage/rent $ _____
Property taxes $ _____
Homeowners insurance $ _____

Transportation
Car payment $ _____
Car insurance $ _____
Fuel $ _____

Utilities
Electricity $ _____
Water $ _____
Phone home and cell $ _____
Internet $ _____
Cable/satellite $ _____
Garbage $ _____

Medical/Health
Life insurance $ _____
Disability insurance $ _____
Health insurance $ _____

Personal/Daily Living

Tithe $ _____

Student loan $ _____

Extra Expenses Paid By Credit card(s) $ ____

Food (grocery store, eating out) $ ___

Entertainment $ _____

Federal/state income taxes $ ____

The Post-It Note

A quick way that Tracy and I stay on top of our expenses is by using a Post-It note. In our checkbook (we share an account which is another key to financial success as a couple) we have a list of the major monthly expenses that come out of our checks along with the amount and date they are paid. Here is an example:

1st Tithe	$100
1st Mortgage	$1,000
5th Roth IRA	$200
10th Satellite	$100
12th Phones/Internet	$200
25th Electric bill	$150 (avg.)
25th Water	$50 (avg.)

This enables us to quickly see how we stand on any given day. For example, if it is November 9th, we know we still have to pay the satellite, phone, internet, electric and water bills. This has helped us keep track of our money in a quick and easy way.

Another way we utilize this Post-It note is by deducting our expenses before we spend our monthly money. One of the nice things about being a teacher is getting paid at the end of the month. This makes it easier to budget since you know exactly when the check is coming in and how much it will be. So let's use the above numbers in this example. If you total them, my monthly expenses add up to $1,800. We will say my monthly take home pay is $2,800. Before the month gets going, I would subtract $1,800 (my monthly expenses) from $2,800 (my take home pay) to get $1,000. I would then take that $1,000 and divide it by four (the number of weeks in a typical month; if the month happens to have 5 weeks in it, I would divide $1,000 by 5) to get $250. I now know how much I have to spend each week without going over my budget.

Track Your Spending

Congratulations! Now that you have listed all of your major expenses, you know where a majority of your paycheck is going. Next we are going to find out what the rest of it is being spent on. I will give you a little heads-up: this one won't be as easy as writing down your major expenses. This one is going to take a lot more time and effort but you will be happy you did it.

You are going to track your spending for one month. I am somewhat old fashioned so when Tracy and I did this, we used pen and paper. I know many of you would prefer to use an electronic device. That is completely fine; no matter how you do it, the important part is that you do. This monthly tracking includes anything you spend money on: from that candy bar to the night at the movies. Write down or type everything you purchased.

Once the month has passed, you will be able to sit down and see exactly where your hard-earned money went. The numbers don't lie: you either wrote or typed them yourself. You will now be able to see exactly where every dollar you earned went. Too many of us spend money on things we truly don't need. As an educator, I am sure you would like to add a little more to your income. There are three ways to make more money: get a higher-paying job, get a second job, or cut back on your spending. Option A would require us to leave the teaching profession. If you feel it is time for a change, then I say go for it. However, most of you are educators for a far bigger reason than just a paycheck and leaving the profession is not something you want to consider. Option B is definitely possible but with all the mandates you now have placed on you, this would be pretty tough. This leaves us with Option C: changing your spending habits. Options A and B both require time to look for another job and are dependent on someone hiring you. Option C is something that can be done today and requires action by just you and your partner.

Cash Is King

To help your money go a little further, you might want to implement a cash-only system for impulse purchases. These include items in the entertainment and eating categories because we can easily overspend in these areas if we are not careful. Items such as electricity and fuel for your automobile(s) are not considered impulse purchases because we only spend what we need in these areas. I have never seen anyone pay the electric company extra or fill up the trunk of their car when their gas tank is full.

Tracy and I did this early in our marriage and it helped us greatly. After we knew how much we needed for our weekly expenses (these included groceries and entertainment) we would pull that exact amount from an ATM machine every Friday. This would be the money to get us until the next Friday.

This could get tricky at times. Let's say it was Thursday

and we had no money left. Friends might call and ask if we wanted to go out to dinner with them. We had to be resolute and say no, and ask if we could take a rain check. By doing this, though, we were sticking with our plan and staying within our budget. I will also warn you that it might take you a couple weeks to determine the amount you need. If you find yourself needing to adjust this number a bit don't become discouraged; handling money correctly is a marathon, not a 50-meter dash. There are numerous advantages to using a cash-only system. Many of us have an emotional attachment to those crisp, green bills. We know how early we got up and how long we worked on lesson plans to earn them. This makes it much harder to part with them compared to just swiping a piece of plastic through a machine. In fact, there are studies that show you will spend 12-18 percent less when using cash instead of plastic.[a]

Using credit cards can not only affect how much you spend but what you choose to buy, too. According to the study "Do Payment Mechanisms Change the Way Consumers Perceive Products" from Promothesh Chatterjee and Randall Rose, the intention to pay with either cash or credit can determine whether a consumer concentrates on a product's benefits or its cost, to the point they might choose different products when they know they will be paying with credit. This study shows:

"When (consumers are) exposed to new products and thinking about paying with credit, they tend to focus on the good things about the product — the aesthetics of it, the features that are better than other products they're considering, the sexiness and luxury of it," Rose said in an interview. "That's as opposed to details related to cost, like the price, shipping cost, warranty cost, installation cost and effort."[b]

In an experiment, consumers primed by researchers to

think about credit cards had trouble recalling facts about a digital camera's cost. In another, those who were thinking about credit were able to correctly identify more words related to the benefits of a laptop computer but fewer about its cost. The opposite was true for those primed to think about paying with cash.

The authors note that this might happen because consumers from an early age are exposed to credit card advertising. This advertising links use of credit cards with highly desirable products and lifestyles, as well as immediate gratification.

Another advantage of using cash is the time you will save. Many of you have extremely hectic lives trying to balance your teaching with getting the kids to practice and putting dinner on the table. Sometimes we might even forget to balance our checkbooks. This can lead to costly overdraft fees. Taking a set amount of cash out once a week can save you a lot of time since there is just one transaction to write down and balance in your checkbook.

A final reason that using cash is beneficial is that it can save you money. Even though our economy is doing better than it was a few years ago, some stores are still struggling. If you use cash, you can take advantage of this. I had a friend who was in the market for a television set with a retail price of $1,000. I told her to walk into the store with $700 cash and see what would happen. After a few minutes of negotiating, she got this set for the $700 she walked in with. It never hurts to ask. The worst the salesperson can tell you is no. Go ahead and try it yourself. Nothing ventured, nothing gained.

Work With Your Partner

According to a recent survey, 22 percent of divorces are directly related to money issues.[c]

I feel that my family's success is due in large part to how Tracy and I work together as a team. We set goals for our family and strive to achieve them with each other's support. It's extremely important for a husband and wife to be on the same page with their finances. The following statistics demonstrate this.

According to a survey by ForbesWoman and the National Endowment for Financial Education, 31 percent of people lied to their spouses about money, 67 percent argued over money lies, and 16 percent of these money lies led to divorce.[d]

A Utah State study showed that a couple with $10,000 in debt and no savings is about twice as likely to divorce as a couple with $10,000 in savings and no credit card debt.[e]

A study done by Citibank found that 57 percent of divorced couples said money fights were the primary reason they did not get along.[f]

I know how crazy and hectic life can be sometimes. Between kids, work, and staying on top of our bills, Tracy and I are pretty busy—as are most folks. I couldn't imagine adding money troubles/arguments to the equation. I see why financial problems can lead to divorce; for many it's the straw that breaks the camel's back.

This is why it is so important for you to work together with your partner. Tracy and I never look at it as her or my money: it is OUR money. What is mine is hers and vice-versa. I feel this is one of the reasons that our marriage is so strong; I highly recommend working as a team on everything you face, but especially financial issues.

Plan Your Budget Before the Month Begins

It is very important to **plan** how you are going to spend your money. In my experience, money can be a bit like my kids. If I don't lay down boundaries and tell them how I expect them to behave, I am asking for trouble. The same is true with my money. This is why it is important to plan how you are going to spend your money before you receive it.

I recommend you plan your budget one week before the next month begins. Because many of you are teachers, you know exactly how much you will get paid. Planning how every dollar will be spent will help you get the most from your paycheck.

I have a great tool for you to use to help you prepare your monthly budget. My friends at the website "I Was Broke, Now I'm Not" (see below for web address) have a monthly budgeting tool that makes this pretty easy. Use this tool by inputting the amount you will earn next month (remember, we are planning how we will spend our money **BEFORE** the month begins). Then, list how you will spend every dollar. This includes saving money in an emergency fund and for retirement. As you input these numbers, the calculations are automatically done for you. Telling your money how to behave will ensure that it goes as far as possible. Here is the link to this great tool:

https://www.iwasbrokenowimnot.com/tools-budgeting/

YOUR HOMEWORK

List all of your major expenses so that you know where your money is going.

Write down or use a device to track every dollar you spend for one month (if applicable, have your partner do the same).

Try using cash only for one month and see if this helps you spend less.

Have a finance meeting with your partner to discuss your goals and how you can achieve them.

CHAPTER 4

The School of Financial Freedom

"We choose to go to the moon not because it is easy,
but because it is hard."

JOHN F. KENNEDY

Before we get started, I want to take a minute and warn
you that gaining control of your finances might not be easy.
In fact, it could be one of the most difficult things you ever
do. However, if it were easy, everyone would have a great
marriage, be able to run a marathon, and have millions of
dollars in the bank. It is often through those difficult chal-
lenges that we grow the most.

Financial Freedom

So what exactly is financial freedom? This can mean
many things. For the purpose of this book, I view financial
freedom as having the ability to do what you have been
called to do, no matter what it will cost or how much you
can make by doing it.

Does that excite you? Imagine having enough money to take your family on that dream vacation and paying cash for it. I know most of you enjoy your jobs but if you don't, imagine going to a job that you actually enjoy! I am not sure what financial freedom looks like for you, but my goal is to help you achieve it.

Managing Money Is Like a Game

I know we are all in different grades (more on that in a bit) when it comes to how we are handling our finances, but the following statistics paint a depressing picture:

- In a survey conducted by The Federal Reserve Board, The Fed asked respondents how they would pay for a $400 emergency; 47 percent said they would either cover the expense by borrowing or selling something. If they could not borrow or sell something, they could not come up with this $400.[a]

- Two reports published by the Pew Charitable Trusts found that 55 percent of households didn't have enough liquid savings to replace a month's worth of lost income and that of the 56 percent of people who said they'd worried about their finances in the previous year, 71 percent were concerned about having enough money to cover everyday expenses.[a]

- The American Psychological Association conducts a yearly survey on stress in the United States. This survey found money to be the country's number one stressor with 72 percent of adults reporting having felt stressed about money at least some of the time and nearly a quarter rated their stress as "extreme."[a]

- A Bankrate survey found that only 38 percent of Americans would cover a $1,000 emergency room visit or a $500 car repair with money they had saved.[a]

- In a survey of American finances published by Pew, 60 percent of respondents said they had suffered some sort of "economic shock"—a drop in income, a hospital visit, the loss of a spouse or a major repair—in the past twelve months. More than half struggled to make ends meet after their most expensive economic emergency. Thirty-four percent of the respondents who made more than $100,000 a year said they felt strain as a result of an economic shock.[a]

Just like games, there are rules when it comes to managing money. Rules such as "spend less than you earn" and "don't buy stuff you cannot afford." If you follow such rules, you will make gains in your financial life. If you don't follow these rules, you may still do okay financially, but not for long. You see, every action has a consequence. This consequence may not be felt immediately, but it will be felt at some point. This is where The School of Financial Freedom can help you greatly. It lists the exact grades you need to pass in order to achieve financial freedom.

The School of Financial Freedom

KINDERGARTEN
Know Your Why/Set Goals

In any area of life we want to have success in, we first must have something we are aiming for. Zig Ziglar said, "Lack of direction, not lack of time, is the problem. We all have 24-hour days." This is so true.

When it comes to your money, having goals is extremely important. Unfortunately, many people let their current financial situation dictate the size of their dreams and goals. Don't let this be you! Set your goals and then work to achieve them, no matter where you stand right now. It might take you a while to get there, but that is okay.

Goal setting is the first grade to pass in The School of Financial Freedom because it helps you know **WHY** you want to win with your money! In addition to setting goals, we also need to know why we are setting these goals. You see, many of us are just anxious to get out of debt and handle our money better because we are sick and tired of not winning with our finances. While those are good reasons, they do not define your "why." Your "why" will keep you going during those tough stretches, and trust me, there will be a few tough tests in this school.

Most people can explain what they do; some can explain how they do it; but very few can clearly articulate why. "Why" is not money or profit; those are results. Your "Why" will propel you to financial success faster than anything else because it is rooted to your core, your calling.

Pretty powerful, right? I'll repeat it! Most people can explain *what* they do; some can explain *how* they do it; but very few can clearly explain *why*. Remember, "Why" is *not* money. Your "Why" is always connected to your core, *your calling*, and will bring you closer to financial success than anything.

The reason we need to determine our "Why" is that it helps us understand our values and what is truly important to us. For instance, asking, "Why is money important to me?" reveals desires that we don't usually think about. Asking and answering this question can take us out of our comfort zones, but recognizing why you want to do better with money is a great first step in aligning your financial decisions with your values.

In the book *Man's Search For Meaning*, Viktor Frankl, a Holocaust survivor, wrote: "When you know your why, you can endure any how." We spend most of our lives focused on the how. This is composed of the obligations and stuff we have to do; basically, it's life's to-do list. Many times we forget why we are doing these things; we just try to cross them off our endless list of things we need to get done.

I am not saying these things don't need to get done, but when we focus on the why, we look at these a little differently. You are probably going to stumble at some point while trying to achieve financial freedom. Your why will help you persevere and continue on even though things might be tough.

In addition to knowing our why, we need to know what we are aiming for. Some want to be able to stay home when the kids arrive whereas others want to take great vacations every year. There is no right or wrong answer; it is personal and based on your own individual hopes and dreams.

One of my financial goals is to have $1 million in investments when I retire. I know many people want to become millionaires, but they don't know why. One of my "whys" in this area is to be able to take special vacations with my family regardless of the cost. This came to light a few years ago. At that point, I was teaching special needs students. One of my students was too sick to attend school so two afternoons per week after school dismissed, I went to his house to teach him. I got paid extra for doing this. I did not count this money as part of our income; I just threw it into a jar and let it accumulate.

After a year, I decided to count it. It added up to a good amount and Tracy and I decided to do something special for our girls: we took them to Disney World! This was so much fun, and I loved every minute of it. One of the things

I would like to do is be able to take my future grandchildren there every year. In order to do this, we must have a sizable nest egg waiting for us when we retire. This is one of my "whys" for investing in my Roth IRA every month. I could come up with a bunch of other ways I could use this money before retirement, but because I have a powerful "why" I continue to invest instead.

I have heard it said that people lose their way when they lose their why. Knowing your why sets you up for success.

FIRST GRADE

Get Health, Automobile and Homeowner's/Renter's Insurance

This grade doesn't need too much explanation. Many of us have heard horror stories of those who were not properly insured.

Being properly insured is an important part of your financial plan, perhaps the MOST important part! I know no one likes to pay insurance premiums (myself included). We think of other things we could be doing with that money. I hate to be the bearer of bad news but bad stuff is going to happen! You or a family member will get sick. Your roof will leak. You may have a fender bender. You can pretend none of these will happen but that doesn't change anything except that you won't be adequately prepared when one of these events does happen. Insurance protects you when life happens.

What is the purpose of insurance? Insurance eliminates the risk of unpredictable and uncontrollable bills by converting them into a predictable and affordable series of insurance payments. Insurance transfers risk from you to the insurance company. It is as simple as that.

It is important to be properly insured. However, you

can also be wasting money and be overly insured. Here are some insurance policies I would recommend you steer clear of:

Cancer Insurance
Accidental Death Insurance
Mortgage Life Insurance
Credit Card Insurance

All of these policies play on your emotions. What if you die in an accident? How will your spouse pay the bills? That is where your term life insurance comes into play. What if you get cancer? That is where health insurance comes into play. If you really feel the need to purchase these policies, make sure you have the must-need policies in place first.

The importance of having health insurance hit home for me a few years ago. My brother, Kyle, is a very fit and active firefighter. However, it was discovered that he had been born with a hole in his heart, and needed open heart surgery to correct this! I cannot even begin to imagine what his medical bills would have been had he not had health insurance. He turned an unpredictable and uncontrollable bill into a predictable one by paying for health insurance every month.

Like I mentioned above, when we take out insurance, we are transferring risk from us to the insurance provider. For instance, when we take out homeowner's insurance, we pay a fraction of what it would cost to rebuild our house if something were to happen to it. When I lived in Florida, my house was struck by a hurricane. It did some damage and we needed to replace our roof, our back porch, and most of our carpet. Since I had homeowner's insurance, I just paid my premium and the insurance company took care of the rest.

If you are renting, you need to have renter's insurance. Your landlord's policy will not cover your belongings if something were to happen. So, if there were a fire and all was lost, renter's insurance would be the only thing that would replace it.

You can make the proper financial decisions throughout your life and then one slip off a ladder can derail your entire financial future. Many of you already have health, automobile and homeowner's insurance. In the next two grades we are going to discuss insurance that you may not have now but need to get as soon as possible.

SECOND GRADE
Get Disability Insurance

While it is very important to save money in an emergency fund, get out of debt, and save for retirement, I think obtaining the protection we will talk about in the following three grades are even more important. The first of these is disability insurance.

Think of disability insurance as paycheck insurance. If you became disabled and were no longer able to work, would you be able to pay all of your bills? This is where disability insurance comes into play.

Many districts offer both short- and long-term disability insurance. Like it sounds, short-term would kick in much sooner than long-term if you became injured and were unable to work. Long-term disability insurance would kick in after a set number of days.

The premiums for short-term coverage are more expensive than for long-term, because the policy pays for the weeks immediately following the injury or illness. My long-term policy would go into effect after 90 days of me being unable to work and will pay me 60 percent of my salary until I am able to collect Social Security. I pay about $20 a month for this coverage. Since we have an emergency fund in place, we could use that for three months if I couldn't work and then start collecting on this policy. If you are just starting out and have nothing saved, you might want to consider signing up for short-term disability so you would start getting paid immediately (make sure you check your individual policy to determine if there a waiting period) rather than having to wait 90 days. However, because this short-term policy costs more, once you have a 90-day cushion, you can sign up for the long-term coverage only and save money each month.

I know we don't plan on becoming injured, but it can happen. What if I was putting up Christmas lights and fell off the ladder and could no longer work? My disability insurance will replace some of my monthly income. In fact, 49 Americans become disabled every minute and three in ten in the workforce today will become disabled before they retire.[b]

This is an important part of your financial plan. Check with your benefits department to see how much this will cost you.

THIRD GRADE
Get Life Insurance

I know this can be a touchy subject because most of us do not like to think about passing away. I have done a lot of research on this topic (all of about ten seconds) and have come up with a great realization. If you are reading this, one day you will die. I don't know when (now that would be scary if I could predict that!) but all we are promised is our last breath.

If you have people that are dependent on your salary to pay the bills, it is important to have life insurance. Life insurance is protection against the loss of income if you pass away and still have financial obligations. Your beneficiary will receive the policy benefit amount. For example, if you had a $100,000 life insurance policy and named your spouse as your beneficiary, he/she would receive that amount if you die.

The goal of life insurance is to provide financial security for your loved ones after you die. Because this is the case, you need to determine your financial situation and how much of your income would need to be replaced if you suddenly passed. For example, do you have young children who need money for college or do you have a lot of debt? If so, you need to have a policy large enough to pay for these expenses. In my case, I have two young daughters who might need money for college, along with weddings. I have a life insurance policy that would enable Tracy to pay off our house, not have to work until the girls became adults, and pay for the girls' college and wedding costs if I were to die.

Many financial experts recommend carrying a policy that is ten times your yearly income. The assumption is that your family could invest this money and, if they earned 10 percent a year on it, replace your income. For example, if you make $50,000 a year and had a life insurance policy of $500,000, your family could invest this $500,000 and, if they earned 10 percent a year, replace your yearly income.

Buying a life insurance policy can be somewhat confusing. There are two basic types: term and whole life. Term insurance is like it sounds: it covers for a stated term such as 10 or 20 years. Whole life usually provides both a death benefit (like term) and a cash savings built into it as well.

With term insurance, you don't get anything back if you continue to live, which is a good problem to have. An easy way to think about term insurance is to compare it to renting a house. The beginning payments are less expensive than owning a house but the rent can increase every few years.

In addition, if you move, you don't get anything back.

A whole life policy is like buying a house. You lock into a certain rate (like a mortgage) and you know exactly what your payments will be. In addition, you are building savings in a whole life policy. If you cash it in before you pass, you will get some money back (just like if you sell your house, you will get the equity you have in it).

The main benefit of term is the price you pay; it's usually much less expensive than whole life. You may have heard of the expression "Buy term insurance and invest the difference." Since a whole life policy costs more, this theory holds that you take the difference between what you are paying for term insurance compared to what you would be paying for whole life and invest this amount.

I have heard the pros and cons of both types of life insurance plans. The most important thing is to make sure you obtain some sort of life insurance to protect your family if they depend on your income to live.

FOURTH GRADE
Get A Will

I know far too many people put off getting a will. It does seem very complicated and a big hassle. Even if your only major possession is your house, you still need a will, as it could take years for the courts to figure out who gets it. If you have minor children, you especially need to get one RIGHT NOW! I mean put this book down and do it. A will details exactly where your children will live in case you die. Do you really want to leave that up to some judge?

You also need to keep in mind that wills are state specific. For instance, when Tracy and I lived in Florida we had a will done there. Upon moving to Georgia, we needed one here to replace the one we had in Florida.

In addition to your will, you also need healthcare power of attorney and a living will. Healthcare power of attorney stipulates the person who will make health decisions for you if you cannot. In addition to obtaining this document, I also think it is a great idea to discuss your wishes with your power of attorney. The living will spells out exactly what you want done if you were in a position that you were alive but could not communicate and needed machines to keep you from passing. When we were in Florida, there was a case in which a woman was in a coma and pretty much non-responsive. Her husband said her wishes were to be allowed to die but her parents said no. She ended up living in this state for 15 years.[c] A living will would have spared her loved ones more anguish than they were already facing.

I know these forms might seem expensive but I have some great news for you. You can obtain all of these for under $40! Dave Ramsey has a bundle on U.S. Legal Forms that includes a state-specific will, a living will, and a power of attorney. Here is the link:

http://www.uslegalforms.com/dave/?homedave

I will admit these forms can be a little complicated to complete, but you can do it. I would suggest finding a time when the kids are asleep and you can concentrate fully on them. You will need to have portions of these notarized, but most banks offer this service.

Before ordering this bundle, I called around to some local attorneys to ask about setting up a basic will and the lowest quote I got to do this was for $250. So even though you will have to spend some time completing this information yourself, you can save a lot of money *and* leave a lasting legacy to your family and loved ones.

FIFTH GRADE
Save One Month of Expenses

Having saved money provides margin. What is margin? It is space. Financial margin creates space. I recommend you begin to create this margin by saving one month of expenses. You may not get to this point in one month but start small. Let's say you are able to find a way to save one-fourth of this amount. Do this for four months and, violà, there is your starter emergency fund. This amount will not cover a major emergency but could pay for those minor, unexpected things that happen such as your heat going out or needing new tires on your car. You will eventually add more to this fund but starting off by saving one month of expenses is a great step in the right direction.

Don't be concerned with earning interest on this money; it is there to help you avoid paying interest. You should have easy access to this money and be able to get it at a moment's notice. You don't want to have it in a place where you'll be tempted to use it for non-emergencies but you also don't want it to be locked up in a CD where you might have to pay a penalty in order to have access to it. Tracy and I have our emergency fund in a savings account at our local bank. This has worked well for us.

SIXTH GRADE
Invest $100/Month for Retirement

We will get into the magic of compound interest in greater detail later on, but it is so important to start investing as soon as possible to take advantage of this magic so that we can achieve some of those goals we listed way back in kindergarten.

I think it is extremely important to get out of debt as

fast as you can, so saving money for something that could be 40 years away might not make much sense to you. I completely understand that point, but let me explain why I think you need to save for retirement as soon as possible, even before tackling your debt.

Many have the best intentions to get out of debt, but for one reason or another, just don't manage to do this. They then get to a point where they want to retire but cannot, because they have nothing saved for these years. In addition, they still have some debt. That is no good! I would like you to start off by just investing a small amount in your retirement account: $100 a month. This may sound like a lot to start with but it really is not much of a sacrifice. If you invest this in a 403(b) (more on the different types of retirement accounts later on) this money is invested pre-tax. This means that $100 would only equal a $75 paycheck difference if you are in the 25 percent tax bracket (if you did not invest this $100, it would be taxed before you were paid and, thus, it would equal only $75 more in your check). If you are a beginning teacher, I want you to do this before you have a chance to get used to your full monthly check. If you are a veteran teacher, this loss in income may be a little more noticeable, but it amounts to less than $3 a day!

To show you why it is so important to begin investing as soon as possible, let's take a look at two friends we will call John and Robert. John got a head start on Robert and began investing $2,000 a year for eight years starting when he was 19 years old. His investments averaged 12 percent growth per year. After eight years, when he was 26 years old, John stopped contributing but his investments still grew at an average rate of 12 percent per year. In all, he invested $16,000.

It took Robert a little bit longer to start investing and he did not begin to do so until he was 27 years old. However, like his friend, Robert contributed $2,000 a year and averaged 12 percent growth on his investments. He did this until he turned 65, so he invested a total of $78,000.

When they both turned 65, John and Robert decided it was time to retire. You may realize this is a trick question but take a guess at who has more in their retirement account: John, who invested a total of $16,000 over eight years, or Robert, who invested a total of $78,000 over 39 years.

Let's take a look:

AGE	John Invests	Value After Interest	Robert Invests	Value After Interest
19	$2,000	$2,240	$0	$0
20	$2,000	$4,749	$0	$0
21	$2,000	$7,558	$0	$0
22	$2,000	$10,706	$0	$0
23	$2,000	$14,230	$0	$0
24	$2,000	$18,178	$0	$0
25	$2,000	$22,599	$0	$0
26	$2,000	$27,551	$0	$0
27	$0	$30,857	$2,000	$2,240
28	$0	$34,560	$2,000	$4,749
29	$0	$38,708	$2,000	$7,558
30	$0	$43,352	$2,000	$10,706
31	$0	$48,554	$2,000	$14,230
32	$0	$54,381	$2,000	$18,178
33	$0	$60,907	$2,000	$22,599
34	$0	$68,216	$2,000	$27,551
35	$0	$76,802	$2,000	$33,097
36	$0	$85,570	$2,000	$39,309
37	$0	$95,383	$2,000	$46,266
38	$0	$107,339	$2,000	$54,058
39	$0	$120,220	$2,000	$62,785
40	$0	$134,646	$2,000	$72,559
41	$0	$150,804	$2,000	$83,506
42	$0	$168,900	$2,000	$95,767

AGE	John Invests	Value After Interest	Robert Invests	Value After Interest
43	$0	$189,168	$2,000	$109,499
44	$0	$211,869	$2,000	$124,879
45	$0	$237,293	$2,000	$142,104
46	$0	$265,768	$2,000	$161,396
47	$0	$297,660	$2,000	$183,004
48	$0	$333,379	$2,000	$207,204
49	$0	$373,385	$2,000	$234,308
50	$0	$418,191	$2,000	$264,665
51	$0	$468,374	$2,000	$298,665
52	$0	$524,579	$2,000	$336,745
53	$0	$587,528	$2,000	$379,394
54	$0	$658,032	$2,000	$427,161
55	$0	$736,995	$2,000	$480,660
56	$0	$825,435	$2,000	$540,579
57	$0	$924,487	$2,000	$607,688
58	$0	$1,035,425	$2,000	$682,851
59	$0	$1,159,676	$2,000	$767,033
60	$0	$1,298,837	$2,000	$861,317
61	$0	$1,454,698	$2,000	$966,915
62	$0	$1,629,261	$2,000	$1,085,185
63	$0	$1,824,773	$2,000	$1,217,647
64	$0	$2,043,746	$2,000	$1,366,005
65	$0	$2,288,996	$2,000	$1,532,166

As hard as it may be to believe, John's investment would outgrow Robert's by more than $700,000! As you can see, John would have $2,288,996 and Robert would have $1,532,166. How does this happen? Starting to invest as early as possible is the key. His $16,000 invested turns into almost $2.3 million. THAT is the power of compound interest!

I know many of you are teachers and most districts don't offer a match when it comes to saving for retirement. However, if your spouse has a job that offers a company match, please take advantage of that.

According to a recent survey conducted by TIAA-CREF, only 77 percent of employees who participate in an employer-sponsored retirement plan contribute enough to receive the full employer match. For employees earning less than $35,000 a year, only 64 percent receive the full match.[d]

These individuals are missing out on a great gift – FREE MONEY!

To illustrate this more clearly, we will say Tom works for a company that matches up to 3 percent the contributions he makes into his 401(k). Tom makes $48,000 a year which would be $4,000/month. Three percent of $4,000 is $120. So Tom would invest $120 each month. The company matches this amount so the total Tom would be investing is $240/month.

Here is where it gets even better. Tom is in the 25 percent income tax bracket. This means his paycheck would be only $90 less each month, because money invested in a 401(k) is done before taxes are taken out. If Tom did not invest this $120, he would only see $90 more in his paycheck (25 percent of $120 equals $30; $120 minus $30 equals $90). So, Tom would be investing $240 (his $120 contribution along with the $120 company match) a month and only miss $90 to do this!

Even if Tom earned 0 percent on his investments, he will be making money. In one year, he would have invested $1,080 ($90 per each of 12 months) but would have $2,880 in his retirement account! If Tom did this for 30 years, he would have invested a total of $32,400 and have $86,400 in his account. This is assuming he earned nothing on his investments!

What if Tom's investments averaged 10 percent growth over these 30 years? He will have over $495,000 in his account! That's right – over ten times the amount he invested. All this for $3 a day. For the price of a Diet Coke from a vending machine a day, Tom could have almost half a million dollars in his retirement account. This is why you need to take advantage of a company match if you are ever offered one. Your company will be helping you retire!

SEVENTH GRADE

Eliminate All Debt Except the Mortgage

I had my first girlfriend and break-up in 7th grade. In The School of Financial Freedom, 7th grade is the year in which we break up with someone we have probably been dating a long time: DEBT!

Some of the common types of debt we focus on here include credit card balances, car loans, student loans, furniture, and debts owed to family and friends.

This requires some discipline and determination but the pay-off is well worth it. When you can keep more of your hard-earned money instead of paying someone else, you will find you can live on a lot less. In addition, when you use the money you have been paying someone else and instead pay this same money to yourself, you can build up a huge margin and begin to see how those goals you set in kindergarten can become a reality.

I have done financial presentations teaching these steps during which people sometimes ask, "Doesn't it make more sense to pay off debt before starting an   emergency fund?" The answer is absolutely! From a mathematical standpoint, it makes much more sense to pay off a debt with a 24 percent interest rate than it does earning 1 percent on your money in a savings account. However, if we are in debt, we have to remember that the math probably didn't get us there. Most of us know it's not wise to buy things on credit but did so anyway.

Let's take a look at the outcome if you pay off your debt

first rather than saving anything in an emergency fund. You are plugging along and doing a great job; in fact, you have already paid off two credit cards. One cold winter morning you go to start your car and the battery is dead. You don't have any money so how in the world are you going to pay for this? Yep, you guessed it, back on the credit card it goes. Many people already feel they can't handle money and here is yet another blow to their self-esteem. At this point, a lot of us might throw in the towel and revert back to our old spending habits. It can be very tempting to skip a grade, but don't! Just like when you attended school, each grade of the School of Financial Freedom teaches you important lessons to help you achieve financial success.

Remember, many of the mistakes we make with our money are based on our behavior. Like losing weight, we know what to do. However, what looks good in writing can often be difficult in the real world. This is why paying off your debt in order from least to greatest works so well: we are focusing on our behavior and rewarding it with positives so that we will want to keep making progress.

EIGHTH GRADE

Save at Least Three Months of Expenses

I realize that three months of expenses may sound like a huge number but let's take a look and see how quickly this can be accomplished. Let's say you needed $3,000/month to live before advancing to this grade. You already saved up one month of expenses in 5th grade. You might think you now need to save $6,000 more to have a total of three months of expenses saved. Hold up! Suppose you have been paying $500/month towards your debt while you were in 7th grade. Once this debt is gone, this money is no longer an expense. In fact, you just reduced your living expenses by $500 a month! Now you just need $2,500 a month to pay for all of your expenses. To cover three months of expenses, you will only need to save $7,500. You already have $3,000 saved so you need to save $4,500 more to have three months of expenses saved. You can now pay yourself the $500 monthly amount that used to go towards your debt. If you do this for nine months, you will have three months of expenses saved!

While the goal in 8th grade is to save at least three months of expenses, I did include the words "at least." Should you aim for more than three months of expenses saved? That is somewhat of a personal question, but I have never talked to someone who said, "Man, I wish I didn't have so much in my savings account." Why would you want to save more? I know you feel pretty secure in your teaching job and, unless you do something really off the wall, will probably not get fired. However, with the recent economic mess our country went through, some districts had to lay off teachers. This was a sad situation for them and I would feel devastated if this happened to me. It would be much worse if I did not have anything saved for a situation like this. Having this margin in place will enable you to sleep peacefully at night. If the unimaginable happened and you lost your job, you would know that you will continue to have a roof over your head, food to eat, and be able to live life for a period of time without having to work. This will also enable you to take some time and catch your breath. Losing a job is a big life event. You will have some time to process this and then look for another job that you actually would want to have and not just rush into the first thing you see advertised.

Remember, you also want this money to be sufficiently accessible. In addition, this money is meant to be used for emergencies and not to earn a lot of interest. We can be a little more aggressive with the money we invest for our retirement which just happens to be included in the next grade.

NINTH GRADE
Invest 15 percent of Your Salary for
Long-Term Dreams

With at least three months of savings in place and no debt except the mortgage, you can begin investing 15 percent of your salary to achieve some of those goals you set in kindergarten.

You already started investing $100 a month when you were in 6th grade. You are going to increase it now to represent 15 percent of your gross income. The beauty is, you can use the money you freed up in 7th grade to do so. We will discuss investing in more detail later on in this book but investments can include mutual funds, stocks, real estate, or perhaps even starting your own business.

If you are a teacher in Georgia, you are already setting aside 6 percent each month into the Teacher Retirement System (TRS). We will discuss in Chapter 8 how TRS works, but we are not even going to include that as part of our investments here. I want you to aim to save as much as possible, and if you are advancing through the grades of the School of Financial Freedom in order, you should have no problem investing 15 percent of your salary once you reach 9th Grade. I have never heard a retired person say, "Gosh, I wish I hadn't invested as much as I did."

TENTH GRADE
Pay off Your Mortgage

The mortgage is the other debt we will discuss in more detail later on. If you are just starting school, getting to 10th grade can seem pretty daunting. The great thing is, it may not even take you ten years to make it here! When you are at this point, the only debt you will have is your house. When this is the case, it can be paid off pretty quickly.

ELEVENTH GRADE
Invest 30 percent of Your Salary for Long-Term Dreams

Think about this for a minute: if you have no debt at all, including your house, wouldn't it be pretty easy to invest 30 percent of your income? We spend so much of our earnings paying other people. Once we eliminate all of our debt, we can easily invest 30 percent and still have plenty left over to live generously, fund our dreams, and do whatever we want!

When we make it to 11th grade, part of this 30 percent can be saving for your child's college fund. Notice, I list saving for your child's college in 11th grade and not Kindergarten! As teachers, we are used to putting others and their needs way before ours. In fact, we often take care of everyone else before even thinking about taking care of ourselves. However, it is so important to take care of your own financial situation before trying to help others.

Let's say you decided to invest for your children's college before investing for your retirement. In fact you did so well, they are able to attend elite Ivy League schools. You are able to cover all of their college expenses in full and they graduate and get great jobs. They then marry and begin having children of their own. You are now getting older and ready to retire but cannot because you haven't saved enough. One day the superintendent announces there will be some severe budget cuts and you are let go. What will you do now?

Unfortunately, many parents get into this situation and have to move in with their children. I am sure Ava and Ella both love me dearly, but I don't want to put them in such a situation. It is my goal to be able to pay for their college, but I am not sacrificing my retirement to do so. They could do well in high school and earn a scholarship. They might have to work during college or not live in the best dorm. At the very worst, they may have to get a student loan. I don't want them to have to get a loan but at least they have that option; the last time I checked, there is no option for a retirement loan.

Think about it – there is a 100 percent chance you will retire one day unless you die before this time. However, there is only a 69 percent chance that your children will go to college.[e]

I know we all think our kids will go to college (as teachers, most of us feel this way) but the statistics do not lie.

Many of us, as parents, feel it is OUR responsibility to pay for all of our child(ren)'s college expenses. In fact, 53 percent of parents said they would prefer to tap their retirement savings rather than have their child take out a loan to pay for college.[f]

Don't fall for this line of thinking. Remember, your retirement should always come before saving for your child's education.

Speaking of college, planning for it can be confusing given all the options available. You can save for college by investing in ESAs (Educational Savings Accounts), 529s and even Roth IRAs. I highly recommend you talk this over with your financial advisor so that you can choose the best option for your child(ren).

When planning for college, think about the value you're getting for your money. As a schoolteacher, I would make the same amount whether I have a degree from Yale or from the University of Georgia. According to the College Board, a "moderate" college budget for an in-state public college for the 2014–2015 academic year averaged $23,410 and one at a private college averaged $46,272. These amounts took into account tuition, fees, housing, meals, books, supplies, and personal and travel expenses.[g] With two daughters who will be graduating from high school in the next nine years, I am thinking like many of you: WOWSERS! This is why it is so important to really think long and hard about college. We can no longer send our kids away and give them time to discover themselves. It is way too expensive for that.

I attended a community college for two years then graduated with my bachelor's degree from a state university and no one has ever held this against me. There are degrees from some universities that mean more than from others but, in many careers, a degree is a degree no matter where one attended.

If you are not able to set enough aside to pay for your child's entire post-secondary education and he has to resort to student loans to help with this, please advise your teen how these work.

Many college students do not work, so they borrow enough to pay for their living expenses as well as tuition and other student fees. I encourage you to explain to her that she will have to start paying towards this loan once she graduates, when she is just starting out in life and will have many other expenses to worry about. If your child does need to obtain a student loan, my advice is that she uses it for educational expenses only and gets a job to pay for her living expenses.

In fact, student loan debt is now something that could have severe consequences for our economy. Nearly 50 percent of young Americans begin their working lives with student debt and 43 million Americans have student loans! The total amount of outstanding student loan debt is $1.3 trillion. This comes at a time when the job market is not as strong as in years past.

According to a study conducted by the Global Financial Literacy Excellence Center, many borrowers are now struggling to make their student loan payments and regret borrowing money for their college expenses. In addition, most borrowers did not fully understand what they were taking on when they obtained student loans. Fifty-four percent of student loan-holders did not try to figure out what their monthly payments would be and 53 percent said that if they could go back in time, they would do things differently when it came to student loans.[h]

Student loan debt could force many younger adults to delay important milestones many of us reach, such as getting married, buying a house, and having children. This leads to a slowdown in the housing market, which can affect many of us. Getting a college degree can be very important. Despite this, if you are unable to fund your child's post-secondary education, help her be smart about college debt or she will find herself in the same spot many are in today.

TWELFTH GRADE
*Do Whatever You Want and Live a
Prosperous Life*

Ok, let's take a moment to pause and dream big right now. Think how nice it will be to walk across that stage and receive your diploma! You are now in the position to do almost anything you want. Let's say you go to work one

Monday morning, and you have just had enough. You know in your heart it isn't what you are meant to do. Guess what? You are now in a position to do whatever you want! Since you don't have any debt, you are now in the position where you can look for something else to do, even if it doesn't pay as much as your current job. You can also save up fast and take that dream vacation you have always wanted to go on. The options for having fun are almost unlimited.

You can also continue to have your money grow. You will have a lot more now to invest. You can also save enough money every month to purchase a house outright and then rent it out. This would bring in income every single month and build your net worth.

However, the greatest thing you will be able to do is bless others. I am not a big fan of others telling me I have to give them some of my hard-earned money, but it feels much differently when you are able to willingly give. Picture yourself stopping at a restaurant and your server is a single mom working to support her family. Think about how cool it would be to leave her a $100 tip! Think of how many families you could bless at Christmas. The list of ways you can truly leave a legacy is endless.

In my life, I am eternally grateful to my Great-Great Uncle Jimmy and my grandmother, who we call Meno. When Uncle Jimmy passed away in the early 90s, he left Meno a relatively small sum of money. Since she was investing already and had money saved for retirement, she could have spent this inheritance on whatever she wanted. Instead of blowing this money, Meno used it to help pay for some of my college expenses. She also used some of it to help my brother, Kyle, attend fire school and become a firefighter. Thanks to these unselfish acts, I was able to become a teacher and have had an impact on hundreds of children and now adults. Kyle was able to become a fireman and paramedic and save countless lives. In fact, Kyle was even appointed Battalion Chief at the young age of 37. I know this brings Meno great joy, and I feel that Uncle Jimmy is smiling down on us, knowing he is still making this world a better place.

Important Components of Your Financial Plan

In the next three chapters, we are going to take a look at three of the most important components of your financial plan: building an emergency fund, getting out of debt, and saving for retirement. Get your Number 2 pencils ready and let's go.

YOUR HOMEWORK

Determine which grade in The School of Financial Freedom you are in according to the following schedule.

The School of Financial Freedom

Kindergarten	Know Your Why/Set Goals
1st Grade	Get Health, Automobile, and Homeowner's/Renter's Insurance
2nd Grade	Get Disability Insurance
3rd Grade	Get Life Insurance
4th Grade	Get a Will
5th Grade	Save One Month of Expenses
6th Grade	Invest $100/Month for Retirement
7th Grade	Eliminate All Debt Except the Mortgage
8th Grade	Save at Least Three Months of Expenses
9th Grade	Invest 15 percent of Your Salary for Long-Term Dreams
10th Grade	Pay off Your Mortgage
11th Grade	Invest 30percent of Your Salary for Long-Term Dreams
12th Grade	Do Whatever You Want and Live a Prosperous Life

The Emergency Fund/Savings Account—Prepare for Those Furlough Days

"Revenue is vanity ...
Margin is sanity ... Cash is king."
ANONYMOUS

"Saving" means to do without something today so that you will have money to spend in the future. It requires you to live differently than many people. Many have little or no money saved because it requires one to deny themselves something they really want right now, to make it possible to have money available for later. To make it even more difficult, you often don't even know how you will use that saved money. In addition, we live in a culture of "I see it, I want it, and I buy it" so it can be really difficult to put anything aside. Since this is the case, far too many spend their entire checks (and, in some cases, more than what they bring in).

There are two basic ways you can save money: investing it in hopes that it will earn interest and grow (this is done in

6th, 9th and 11th grades in The School of Financial Freedom) or placing it in a savings account that doesn't earn much interest but is there for protection, purchases, and opportunities. This is 5th and 8th grades in the School of Financial Freedom. That is what we are going to focus on in this chapter.

Where Does It Go

To start off, remember that we are not trying to earn a lot of interest on our emergency funds; funds for growth is the money you invest in 6th, 9th and 11th grades in The School of Financial Freedom. An emergency fund should be in a place that is easily accessible, but not so easy that you will be tempted to spend it. You can simply use a money market savings account at your bank. Ally Bank and Capital One 360 also offer great savings accounts. This type of account allows you to write checks from it or transfer money online from it into your checking account with a few clicks.

How to Save

To be successful at saving money, consider employing a strategy known as "pay yourself first." You see, most of us pay ourselves last. We pay other people for all of our expenses and then having nothing left over for ourselves. Why do you think the government takes taxes out of our paychecks before we receive them? Could you imagine if they waited and asked us to pay them what we owe every April? As staggering as our national debt is, I am sure it would be much higher!

Establish an automatic transfer from your paycheck into your savings account. Pretend this money is not even there. Make it a habit to continuously save a set amount or percentage of your income and put this into a savings account every month; over time, you will have a huge umbrella to protect you during those rainy days!

Why Is It Important

Saving is important for five main reasons. First, saving covers emergencies. It provides security for unexpected events like having a major repair or a sudden illness. This way you have money to draw from so that you can continue to advance through the School of Financial Freedom. Second, when you continue to save, you should be able to buy a car, furniture, etc. without having to use credit and possibly pay interest on the purchase. Third, savings will enable you to pay for those known, upcoming non-monthly expenses. Fourth, savings can enable you to take advantage of opportunities that come your way and provide a pool of resources to make your hopes and dreams become a reality. Finally, savings provides protection in case you lose your job.

Five Ways a Savings Account Can Help You

1. Emergencies

No one expects something bad to happen but sometimes life throws us a curveball. I was reminded of this recently. We were enjoying one of those picture-perfect fall family days. We decided to get some frozen yogurt. While we were enjoying our treats, our girls started doing gymnastics. Out of the blue, Ava slipped and broke her arm! We had to rush her to the local emergency room, and they had to put a cast on it. Even though we have good health insurance, we still had a co-pay of $150 for this ER visit. I definitely wasn't planning on this expense, but it was not a big deal because we had an emergency fund. It was such an emotional day (all parents know what I'm talking about when you can't make your baby feel better), and I am so glad we were able to solely focus on Ava and not stress about the bill.

2. Purchases

I know some people say they just have bad luck and something always seems to go wrong. The truth is, luck really has nothing to do with it. If you live in a house long enough, something will break. If you drive a car long enough, something will need to be repaired. If you have kids, they will break something: either an object or a body part. It is called life.

This past year, we experienced this first-hand. First, our garage door suddenly stopped working. We had a repair company come out and we needed new springs and a few other things. The total came to a little over $900. Six months later, I needed repairs on my car that totaled $800. Three months after that, at the beginning of summer, our air conditioning unit went out and we had to purchase a new unit. That cost us $4,000. Then, one week later, Tracy's car needed repairs which totaled another $1,000! Because we had planned for such unexpected events and had ample savings, we were able to pay for these in cash and move on with our lives. There were no future credit card bills that would follow us for months; we simply wrote a check and were done with it.

I know many think that having payments is just a way of life. That does not have to be the case. If you build up your savings account, you can pay for most of your purchases outright and move on with your life.

3. Known Upcoming Non-Monthly Expenses (KUEs)

Saving money every month for your KUEs is something I learned from my friend Joe Sangl, President of *I Was Broke. Now I'm Not.* These can also be called budget-busters because that is exactly what they will do. These expenses seem to appear at the last minute and the most inopportune times because we have not prepared for them even though we knew they were coming.

For instance, Christmas comes every December 25th without fail. However, many people fail to prepare for the expenses associated with this holiday and turn to debt to buy presents for their loved ones. This causes them to lose some, if not all, the progress they have made the previous eleven months of the year with their finances.

You can save for your KUEs by making them an "every paycheck" expense. The first step is to identify all of your upcoming non-monthly expenses. Here is a list of common KUEs:

Real Estate Property Taxes
Life Insurance Premiums
Auto Insurance Premiums
Car Repairs and Maintenance
Home Repairs and Maintenance
Health Club Fees
Golf Club Fees
Professional Organization Dues
Vacations
Income Taxes
Weddings
Christmas
Birthdays
Anniversaries
Graduations

College Expenses
Car Replacement
Furniture Replacement

This list could go and on. The most important thing to remember is these expenses are both KNOWN and UPCOMING. There should be no surprises. The great thing is that saving for these KUEs is not that difficult. You must have discipline to set aside money each paycheck but you will be so happy that you did.

For instance, let's say you plan to spend $1,200 on Christmas. If you save $100 a month starting in January, you will have $1,200 by December. Think about how nice it will be using CASH for Christmas! Because you saved for it in advance, this holiday won't follow you until the following June in the form of credit card bills!

Just like a mortgage company will put money for your property taxes and homeowner's insurance into an Escrow account, you can calculate the amount you need to save each paycheck for these expenses and create an Escrow account for them.

To show you an example, we are going to say you get paid once a month. You want to have the following amounts for your KUEs:

Christmas	$1,000
Vacation	$1,500
Property Taxes	$1,200
Health Insurance Deductible	$2,500
Car Repairs	$800

When we add these together, we get a grand total of $7,000. We take this $7,000 and divide it by 12, the number of paychecks you will receive in a year if you are paid monthly. This equals $583. Now we break this down into the KUE subcategories we have listed. So every month we put $83 into our Christmas Fund, $125 into our Vacation Fund, $100 into our Property Taxes Fund, $208 into our Health Insurance Deductible Fund and $66 into our Car Repairs Fund.

See how this can help you? By turning these non-monthly expenses into monthly ones, you have dramatically lessened the impact they will have on your budget. For instance, when it is time for vacation, you will already have $1,500 saved for it!

Here are some tips when calculating your KUEs:

- Recalculate these at least once per year.
- Don't forget to add long-term expenses such as weddings and vehicle replacement.
- Make your savings for these automatic.

4. Funding Hopes and Dreams/Taking Advantage of Opportunities

I do feel people are correct when they say that the rich get richer and the poor get poorer. First, rich people continue to do the same actions that helped them accumulate money in the first place and poor people continue to do the same things that made them broke.

Another reason this occurs is that rich people have money set aside to take advantage of opportunities that arise. I was reminded of this when I decided to publish my first book, *How to Survive (and Perhaps Thrive) on a Teacher's Salary*. At that point in my life, I was a school teacher and that was it. I was not a writer in any way, shape, or form. As I mentioned before, I had to pay almost $4,000 to have my first book published; but it was well worth the cost.

My books have given me many opportunities. There are also other doors out there that I have no clue exist yet but will possibly open for me because of what I have been able to accomplish. However, none of this would have ever happened if I did not have any money to invest in myself. I have heard luck defined as when opportunity meets preparation. Please start preparing your savings account so that you, too, can take advantage of the opportunities that will come your way.

5. Changing Jobs/Job Loss

I felt a calling to help others manage their money better. A couple of years ago I was offered the chance to do this. I actually took a slight cut in pay from what I was making teaching, but was so glad that I was able to take advantage of this opportunity. I had some positive results and was rewarded with a greater than 40 percent raise before a year ended. However, we never got used to living up to this salary.

The following year I was offered the chance to help others manage money in churches throughout the country but this job had one catch—I had to take greater than a 25 percent pay cut! Because we had never gotten used to living up to my higher salary, I was able to take this job that I felt He was calling me to do.

After having this job for seven months, I was laid off. The company did not grow as expected and I was no longer needed. This is where our savings helped us so much. I cannot begin to explain how difficult this was to my psyche. As a man, I feel like I need to be the provider for my family. Because this is the case, I was ready to take the first opportunity presented to me. Two days after being let go, I actually had a job offer to teach at a school that was over an hour from home. I was strongly considering it, but Tracy reminded me that we had savings in place and I could take a little longer to make a decision. She knew driving this far every day would not be a good fit for our family. I know it is not common for teachers to get laid off, but sometimes school districts have to make cuts. Having savings in place can greatly help if this happens to you.

A Final Thought on Saving

For an even greater incentive to save, compare the results of spending $100 more than you earn each month for ten years with spending $100 less than you earn each month for ten years. By spending $100 more each month, you will be in the hole $12,000 before interest is even calculated; spend $100 less and you will possess $12,000 before you total the interest earned: a staggering difference of $24,000 at the end of ten years! The difference between sinking into debt and walking on the firm ground of savings is a matter of a few dollars a day.

YOUR HOMEWORK

If you have not already done so, open a savings account and work on building this up to at least one month's worth of living expenses.

CHAPTER 6

Let's Talk About Debt

*"The rich rules over the poor, and the borrower
is the slave of the lender."*

PROVERBS 22:7

It is so interesting that Solomon, considered one of the wealthiest and wisest men to have ever walked Earth, said this thousands of years ago. This was way before credit cards and department stores. However, this same principle that held true thousands of years ago still holds true today and will for many years to come. If you owe someone money, you are basically at their mercy. Borrowing money changes the dynamic of any relationship. It isn't just a simple financial transaction that took place; in essence, the lender controls the borrower.

Even if you borrow money from a family member, the relationship changes. Let's say you owe your favorite uncle $1,000. You have him come over for Thanksgiving dinner but are somewhat ashamed to watch football on that new television set of yours because you know you owe him money and are wondering what he is thinking about this purchase. He may not even be thinking this, but you project it because you feel guilty. When you have financial obligations to someone, these must be considered before making any financial decision. Because this is the case, Solomon is correct: debt does cause a form of slavery in which we are held captive by interest rates, harassing phone calls, or even or own guilt. Is it any wonder that it is called **Master**card?

An American Story

John and Julie started off their marriage like a typical American couple. They met at church and fell in love quickly. They both graduated from college with student loan debt. In fact, they each carried the average balance, a little over $35,000.[a]

Julie is a nurse and makes $36,000 a year. John is a teacher and his annual salary is $35,000. Even though they both majored in fields that do not pay large salaries, they didn't really think about this when obtaining their student loans.

John was so in love with Julie and wanted to make their engagement as special as possible. He only had $500 in savings when they started getting serious. Shortly after that, he knew she was the one. Despite having very little in his bank account, he bought a $10,000 engagement ring. He obtained a store credit card from a jewelry store in the mall and put the entire cost of the ring on that. The payment was interest-free for five years, and he figured he would easily pay it off by then. The minimum monthly payments were only $100 and John figured once they got married, they would combine their salaries and be able to pay extra towards this.

Their engagement was magical. Julie always talked about how her favorite place to visit was Disney World. Yep, you guessed it—John planned a magical day at The Magic Kingdom. In fact, John got down on one knee in front of Cinderella's castle right as the fireworks were going off. Yes, it was like a story book! However, because he didn't have the money upfront to pay for this special day, it all went on the Visa card.

After the engagement, John and Julie began planning for the big day. They did discuss keeping the costs down and possibly having a small ceremony, but because they were both in careers that revolve around people, they had many friends and relatives who *needed* to come to their wedding. Julie's parents agreed to pay for half the cost of this special day, but John and Julie had to pay for the rest of it. As fate would have it, the cost was the average price a couple spends on their wedding, a little over $26,000.[b]

While this was a steep price, John and Julie felt it was worth it. Everyone had so much fun, and they started off their marriage on the right track (at least they thought so at the time). The following day, they flew off to Mexico for a week-long honeymoon spent in the sun. It was one of the best weeks of their lives.

After the honeymoon, they decided to start their future by renting a small apartment. This was going to be temporary, because they had dreams of buying a starter home. However, one month later, the credit card bills (along with the added stress) started to arrive. Their wedding expenses alone totaled $26,000 (this included the cost of the engagement ring, their part of the wedding and the honeymoon). While it sounded like a good idea at the time, they now began to wonder if it had been really worth it. When they added their student loan debt to the credit card debt, they barely had enough to cover their current living expenses let alone a much more costly mortgage payment. Even though they both loved kids and wanted a large family, they couldn't see how it would be possible to support even one child. Once the honeymoon ended, it seemed like the fun did, too.

Most people would agree that this is not a great way to start off a marriage. Unfortunately, many fall into this debt trap and begin their lives already behind the eight ball. I hope your story is not like John and Julie's, but if it is (or you know someone whose life is like theirs) I have some great news for you: life allows us to learn from our mistakes and make a change in the right direction. It will take some work and sacrifice, but this book will show you how it can be done.

What Is Debt

Because many people define debt differently, let's define what I classify as debt before we get started. I consider debt as any obligation owed by one party (the debtor) to another party (the creditor). In simpler terms, debt is any money you owe to someone else. This includes your mortgage (if you have one), your car, student loans, and credit cards.

Unfortunately, borrowing money has become a way of life for many Americans. Credit cards and loans are so common now that a lot of us feel it is our Constitutional right to borrow and charge in the pursuit of happiness. This is accomplished by accumulating more stuff. This stuff is supposed to lead to a better life. In fact, every year new and better stuff is advertised as evidence of living a prosperous life. Even a sacred holiday in which we give thanks for our blessings has now turned into the kick-off of the accumulation season. We leave our loved ones, after stuffing ourselves, to go buy them things that they will forget about by the time

Valentine's Day arrives. To make it even worse, we buy this stuff with money we don't have!

When you are in debt, you have lost some of your freedom. The more debt you have, the less freedom you have. When you are making payments for months, or even years, and the interest on these payments is eating away at your hard-earned money, you are becoming a slave to the lender.

Like we discussed before, most of us get into debt because we are looking to make a quick fix. There is an area of our lives that we are not happy with and we go out and buy something to make us feel better. While this works, the feeling doesn't last. In fact, we usually feel worse after the high has worn off. We then have to go buy something else, and thus, the cycle begins. Gaining control of your debt is far more about your emotions than it is about numbers.

The Debt Fallacy

Unfortunately, our very own economy (if you are a U.S. citizen) is built on debt. As I write this, our national debt is over $20 trillion.[c]

To put this amount into perspective, if you were born on the same day that Jesus was, and spent $1 million every day until today, you would not have spent even $1 trillion.[d]

Our debt is over $20 trillion! In fact, if you spent one dollar per second, in a day you would spend $86,400. Over the course of a year, your spending would come to more than $31.5 million. At that rate of spending, it would take you over 32,000 years to spend one trillion dollars.[e]

I am just pointing out what many of you know. In fact, our government is representative of us. It is of the people, by the people, for the people. Broke people have elected representatives just like them.

Unfortunately, like the people we elect, we get accustomed

to taking on more and more debt. I don't know about you, but I get multiple offers every week from a credit card company wanting me to become a "valuable" card holder. With this constant bombardment, it is actually kind of surprising that we are not in worse financial shape. However, what these very same special offers don't point out is that once we take on debt, we no longer are in control of our time and effort. We now owe someone money, and thus, have to use our manpower and time to earn this money only to turn right back around and pay it to someone else. In addition, oftentimes interest (sometimes lots of it) is added to this amount!

The True Cost of Debt

Many of us accumulate debt on things we really don't need (or for that matter, even really want, except for a brief moment in time) without thinking about the future ramifications. Even though paying the minimum payment looks very affordable, you have to understand the true cost of debt.

It is so easy to swipe a piece of plastic compared to parting with real dollars. We have an emotional attachment to dollar bills because we know how early we got up and how hard we worked to earn them. Plastic does not make us feel the same way. In fact, according to research from USA Technologies, consumers spend 32 percent more per vending machine purchase with credit cards and debit cards than with cash and coin transactions.[f]

In addition, McDonald's reports its average ticket is $7 when people use credit cards versus $4.50 for cash.[g]

There is a reason that many of us get numerous credit card offers in the mail each week, and it is not because we are a valued customer. Once you get behind with debt, it can be a very tough climb out. If someone charges $3,000 on a credit card with an 18 percent interest rate and just pays the minimum amount each month (2.5 percent), it will take over 18 years to get rid of this debt! By the time this is paid off, it will have cost almost $7,000: more than double what was originally borrowed!

Some might think, "I use my credit card wisely and pay it off in full each month. In addition, I get points when using my card. Why should I be worried?" Well, it is great that you pay it off every month, but be careful. Sometimes life gets in the way, and if we are careless we could miss a payment. This would lead to late fees plus having to pay interest. Unfortunately, many people think they are doing well by making the minimum monthly payment on their credit cards. This can destroy their financial future!

To further illustrate why paying the minimum payment can hurt you in the long run, let's say you have a relatively low credit card balance of $500 with an 18 percent interest rate. We will say your credit card company sets your minimum monthly payment at $15. Not too bad, you might think. If you divide this $500 by $15 (the monthly payment), you should have this debt paid off in 34 months ($15 x 34 = $510). While that may sound right, you will actually not pay it off in full until paying this amount for 46 months, rather than 34. How can this be? It's the result of compound interest working against you! If you make this $15 payment for 46 months, when all is said and done, you will have paid $690 ($15 x 46) for your $500 purchase, almost 40 percent more than the original price! This is with only a $500 debt. Imagine if it was $50,000! This is why it is so tough to get out of debt.

For a moment, let's pretend you become so tired of your credit card debt you decide to just stop paying it. The monthly bills come in and you just throw them in the garbage. What happens then?

First, your creditor will most likely contact you if the payment does not arrive by the due date. They may or may not (depending on past payments) charge a late fee. If you ignore this request, your account will become delinquent. This means it is official: you are behind in paying this debt and your creditor reports it to the credit agency. Then, the credit card company will raise your interest rate to the default rate.

If you continue to ignore the monthly bills, the next step is bound to get your attention. Threatening letters will arrive in the mail attempting to get you to respond. You may even start to receive calls from collection agencies when you are trying to enjoy time with your family. If this doesn't make you take notice, you may get sued by the lender. If you continue to keep your head buried in the sand, your creditor might place your account in the charge-off category. At this point, they will not expect to see a dime from you; however, you are still not in the clear. Your creditor will probably sell this debt to another company for a fraction of the amount you owe. This "new" collection agency will begin calling you, asking if you can pay any amount on this debt. They hope they can get anything from you (they made a very small investment on collecting this so even if they get you to pay 10 percent of the balance they will more than likely have made out well).

I haven't even brought up yet the most obvious consequence: the damage to your credit score. A poor credit score will impact the interest rate you are charged on other loans. A spontaneous purchase could haunt you for many years—even decades!

But What About the Points

Some think it is wise to use credit cards for purchases

because of the points they receive. Think about how smart credit card companies are. They "reward" you for going into debt and spending money you don't have! I know of a credit card that enables you to receive $100 back for every $10,000 you spend. When we think of it this way, it doesn't make much sense.

Your greatest asset when it comes to wealth building is your income. Owing others money slows your progress in the School of Financial Freedom. Have you ever heard a millionaire say, "Man, those credit card points were the keys to my financial success"? Me neither!

Good Debt: Is There Such a Thing?

While I don't consider any debt to be good, there is some debt that is necessary for most of us. We usually borrow money to purchase something we don't have the cash for at that particular moment in time. As we just discussed, this will end up costing you more in the long run (sometimes much more) when you add interest to this amount. Although no debt is good, some is worth it because it allows you to make a purchase that will pay off in the long-term.

A good example of this is a mortgage. Most of us (especially school teachers) probably don't have enough money sitting around to buy a house outright. This is where a mortgage comes into play. Over a number of years, a house should appreciate in value. In addition, unless we want to be homeless, we need a place to live. Add to this the fact that interest rates are currently still historically low, buying a house can be an example of necessary debt.

Another example of this type of debt could be a student loan. Now, there are many horror stories out there about the dangers of these loans. However, I bet many of you had a student loan to get your teaching degree. Without this, you would not be in the position you are currently in. I am all for graduating college without any debt, but know that some don't see this as a possible option. For them, a student loan helped them obtain a better paying job than would have otherwise been possible.

While I am on the topic of student loan debt, I wanted to share a personal experience of when this debt can be bad. After giving a financial presentation to a large group of new teachers, I had one ask me a depressing question. She said she had a lot of student loan debt and wanted my advice on paying it off. Now, the definition of "a lot" varies so I asked her exactly how much debt her student loans totaled. I was not prepared for her answer. She said $180,000! Yes, you read that correctly. She owed $180,000 and chose a career in which the starting salary is around $35,000. After taxes are taken out, she could apply every cent she earns towards this debt for six years, and it still would not be paid off! I point this out to reinforce how careful you need to be when taking on debt, even necessary debt.

A final example of good debt is money used for purchasing or starting a business. If this business provides a worthwhile product and is managed well, the company should do well and could become a good investment. The main thing to remember is that with all three of these debts (mortgage, student loan, and business) you are acquiring debt so that it will enable you to earn more money.

If you borrow money to purchase something, the following criteria should be met:

1. The item should be something that will increase in value or produce an income.

2. The value of the item should be equal to or worth more than the amount borrowed to purchase the item.

3. The amount you borrow should be within your ability to repay without placing a strain on your budget.

For example, consider a home purchase. The family home has historically been an appreciating asset which meets our first criteria. If you purchase a house with a decent down payment and use a shorter 15-year loan, its value will be greater than or close to what you owe on it. With the first two criteria met, we consider the third, which is where many people went wrong during the housing crisis in 2009. The house you purchase should not be so expensive that the monthly mortgage payments place a strain on your ability to repay. If you can meet all of the criteria listed above, then the money you borrow can be justified.

While I don't want you to carry any debt at all, I know that being completely debt-free when starting your career is not realistic for most of us, especially teachers. Just remember to try and eliminate this debt as soon as possible. To help you, we are going to discuss a sure-fire way to do this.

The Four Types of Debt

When you think of debt, categorize it into one of these forms: terrible debt, bad debt, better debt, or best debt.

Terrible Debt

Terrible debt is the worst debt of all. This type of debt charges extraordinary interest and is extremely punitive. Examples include payday loans, pawn loan, car title loans, and rent-to-own loans. Avoid this type of debt at all costs!

Bad Debt

Bad debt charges high interest on items that have no value or rapidly drop in value. Examples include credit card and furniture debt.

We have already discussed how destructive credit card

debt can be. What about furniture debt? Many of us see those ads which offer no interest for three years. What can be so bad about that? Let me tell you a little secret about these "deals" that the salesperson doesn't mention. Suppose you purchase furniture to upgrade your living room at a total cost of $5,000. The interest rate is 20 percent, but because the purchase is interest-free for three years, you won't have to worry about it because you know you will have it paid off by then. You do a great job making the monthly payments, and after 36 months owe only $100 on this loan. You are a little disappointed because it isn't fully paid off but you aren't too upset. You reason that because you only owe $100, at the most you will pay $120 if you add the 20 percent interest to this amount. I hate to be the bearer of bad news but you are wrong. You will have to pay 20 percent interest on the original purchase price of $5,000. So you go from owing $120 to owing $1,100! No wonder you see these horrible plans offered all the time.

Better Debt

Better debt is debt that charges reasonable interest rates on items that produce a return on investment. This type of debt increases your net worth or income. Take a guess at an example of better debt. Hint: we discussed this earlier in this chapter. If you said mortgage or student loan debt, you win! These two types of debt usually offer relatively low interest rates. Your house should help you increase your net worth over time and a student loan should help you increase your income.

Best Debt

If one were to have debt, this is the best type! This debt has reasonable interest charges on items that are passed on to someone or something else. Examples of best debt include rental real estate, commercial real estate, and business equipment.

Let's take a look at rental real estate. If you own a home and rent it out to someone else, this person will be paying your mortgage for you! Let's pretend you buy a $120,000 home and put $20,000 down on this. You borrow the remaining $100,000 for 15 years at a 4 percent interest rate. The monthly payment (excluding taxes and insurance) would be about $740. To help cover the taxes and insurance, you rent it out for $1,000. A family decides to rent it and lives there for 15 years. If your house value increased by 1 percent each year, it would now be worth a little over $139,000. You decide to sell it at this point for that amount. You will have made $119,000 from your $20,000 investment (the down payment). I bet you can see why this is the best debt!

Now that we discussed the meaning and types of debt, let's eliminate it once and for all!

YOUR HOMEWORK

Determine which type of debt you have: terrible, bad, better, or best.

CHAPTER 7

Eliminate Your Debt and
Thrive on Your Teacher's Salary

"If you are always trying to be normal, you will never know how amazing you can be."

MAYA ANGELOU

Lose Your Debt

The average American drives a car financed by a bank, on a road financed by bonds, using gas bought with a credit card, on the way to the local mall, and opens a store card there to furnish his bank-owned house with things paid for in an installment plan. Take a moment to read that sentence again. Wow! It is so sad but true!

You see, it is normal to be in debt. When I was in 7th grade, I did my best to be somewhat normal and try to fit in with the popular kids. However, when we are in 7th grade in The School of Financial Freedom, we DO NOT want to be normal. For many, normal means being in debt.

We are now going to discuss a way for you to eliminate your debt so that you are not normal. When we invest our money, we use the power of compound interest to help us build wealth. In fact, investing $100/month could turn into more than $400,000 over time. Even one of the smartest men to ever walk earth had something to say about compound interest. Albert Einstein said, "The most powerful force in the universe is the power of compound interest." If someone as wise as Einstein observed this, I definitely want it working for me!

When you are paying interest, you are actually doing the complete opposite. You are going against the most powerful force in the financial universe. This is why it is so important to eliminate your debt in order to win with your money.

Document Your Debt Reality

Where do we begin? First, we need to calculate how long it will take us to become debt free. We start by listing every non-house and non-business debt we owe. You need to know the following: the name of the debt, how much you currently owe, and the minimum monthly payment. To help illustrate this, we are going to pretend you have the following debts:

Name of Debt	Balance You Owe	Monthly Payment
Credit Card	$5,000	$100
Student Loan	$10,000	$250
Car Loan	$12,500	$300
Total Debt	$27,500	$650

Because you know the importance of not accumulating any new debt (and therefore, won't add to the total), we are just going to use these debts when calculating how long it will take you to eliminate it. We will view these three obligations as one big debt totaling $27,500. We will also add up the total monthly payments on these debts to pretend you are making one big payment. This equals $650. Next, we divide the total debt owed ($27,500) by the overall monthly payments ($650) and we will be debt free in 42.3 months. Now, I know at this point some of you might be asking, "What about the interest?" This a great question because we did not include this in our calculation. There is a reason for this omission. Interest charges will definitely have an impact on eliminating debt. However, many times when people attack their debt with focus and intensity, they actually eliminate it within the calculated time frame and, in some cases, even sooner! In an upcoming chapter, we are going to go over some ways you can speed up this process for you, too!

Eliminate Your Debt

There are two basic debt reduction strategies offered by most financial coaches. One strategy is to focus on debts with the highest interest rates first and eliminate these as quickly as possible. While this makes great mathematical sense, we have to remember that math did not get us into debt. Our financial behavior led to it. The difficult part about this method is the follow through. You see, you might have a high interest debt of $20,000 with a payment of $250/month. It would take you over six years to pay this off! While this is possible, six years is a long time to focus on one debt. Many of us would grow tired, and with one little financial challenge, we would give up. We may just figure we will have a credit card payment forever and not stay focused on paying it off. This is where the other method comes into play: The Debt Snowball. It is my favorite method.

The Debt Snowball

In the debt snowball method, you focus on the smallest debt first and proceed from there. You list debts in order from least to greatest balance owed and just move down the list; remember, we are not focusing on the interest rates with this method, but the balance owed. This works well because of the emotional and noticeable impact. Once you pay off that first debt, you get a morale boost and are motivated to keep going. When you no longer have to write a check for one of the debts, you immediately notice you are making progress! Then you focus on paying off the next debt and the momentum is really rolling now. This is very similar to being on a diet. If you lose two pounds the first week, you realize your hard work and effort are worth it and are motivated to lose even more. Once you get the snowball rolling, it can quickly become an avalanche.

Here are the steps you can take to apply the Debt Snowball to your debt:

- Restructure high interest debt to lower interest rates.

- List your debts from the smallest amount owed to the largest.

- Pay minimum payments on all debts except the smallest amount owed.

- Apply all additional money to the smallest debt.

- When the smallest debt is eliminated, take the monthly payment you were paying for that debt and add it to the monthly payment you are making on the smallest remaining debt.

- Continue this process with intense focus until you are DEBT FREE!

The Debt Snowball in Action

To see how great this is, we need to take a look at how this works in the real world with real numbers. We are not going to list our mortgage debt at this point; that comes later when we are in 10th grade. We are going to list all other debt. So let's say you have the following debts:

Credit Card 1	$5,100
Credit Card 2	$2,900
Car 1	$15,200
Car 2	$12,250
Student Loan	$16,250
Doctor	$1,000

Now we are going to put them in order from least to greatest and list what we pay on each of these debts every month.

Debt Name	Balance	Monthly Payment
Doctor	$1,000	$100
Credit Card 2	$2,900	$100
Credit Card 1	$5,100	$150
Car 2	$12,250	$400
Car 1	$15,200	$500
Student Loan	$16,250	$200
Total Debt	$52,700	$1,450

In this example, you have a total of $52,700 in debt and pay $1,450 towards this every month. Once again we are not calculating the interest, just the actual debt amount owed. If we divide $52,700 by $1,450, you would eliminate this debt in 36.3 months, a little over three years.

Let's see how we can speed that up a bit. Remember, we are going to make minimum payments on all our debts except the one we owe the least amount on. Suppose we free up an extra $100 a month to apply to our smallest debt (only about $3 a day!). This is what our Debt Freedom Date (DFD) calculation now looks like:

Debt Name	Balance	Monthly Payment
Doctor	$1,000	$200
Credit Card 2	$2,900	$100
Credit Card 1	$5,100	$150
Car 2	$12,250	$400
Car 1	$15,200	$500
Student Loan	$16,250	$200
Total	$52,700	$1,550

DFD: 34 months (two years, 10 months)

Because we are tackling the smallest debt first, we apply this extra $100 to the Doctor and continue paying what we have been on the rest of our debts. After five months, the doctor debt will be gone! So this is what our debt picture would look like:

Debt Name	Balance	Monthly Payment
Doctor	PAID	OFF! (Freed Up $200)
Credit Card 2	$2,400	$100
Credit Card 1	$4,350	$150
Car 2	$10,250	$400
Car 1	$12,700	$500
Student Loan	$15,250	$200

Now that we no longer owe the Doctor, we have freed up another $200/month. We are going to continue using the snowball and apply this $200 to the next smallest debt, which in this case is Credit Card 2. We have been paying $100/month on this debt so we will now pay $300/month. Here is how our debts look now:

Debt Name	Balance	Monthly Payment
Doctor	PAID	OFF! (Freed Up $200)
Credit Card 2	$2,400	$300
Credit Card 1	$4,350	$150
Car 2	$10,250	$400
Car 1	$12,700	$500
Student Loan	$15,250	$200
Total	$44,950	$1,550

DFD: 29 months (2 years, 5 months)

If we did this for eight months, one of our credit cards will be paid off! Here is what our debt picture looks like now:

Debt Name	Balance	Monthly Payment
Doctor	PAID	OFF! (Freed Up $200)
Credit Card 2	PAID	OFF! (Freed Up $100)
Credit Card 1	$3,150	$150
Car 2	$7,150	$400
Car 1	$8,700	$500
Student Loan	$13,650	$200
Total	$32,650	$1,250

So what is your next step? You guessed it: we add the $300 we have been paying on Credit Card 2 to what we are paying on the other credit card. So here is what that looks like:

Debt Name	Balance	Monthly Payment
Doctor	PAID	OFF! (Freed Up $200)
Credit Card 2	PAID	OFF! (Freed Up $100)
Credit Card 1	$3,150	$450
Car 2	$7,150	$400
Car 1	$8,700	$500
Student Loan	$13,650	$200
Total	$32,650	$1,550

DFD: 21 months (1 year, 9 months)

Well, seven months later (20 months total), Credit Card #1 is paid off! How great would this feel? In less than two years, you will have paid off three debts with two of those being credit cards! Here is your updated debt picture:

Debt Name	Balance	Monthly Payment
Doctor	PAID	OFF! (Freed Up $200)
Credit Card 2	PAID	OFF! (Freed Up $100)
Credit Card 1	PAID	OFF! (Freed Up $150)
Car 2	$4,250	$400
Car 1	$5,200	$500
Student Loan	$12,250	$200
Total	$21,700	$1,550

Now we can see how this snowball really starts growing! You are going to take the $450 you have been paying on Credit Card #1 and apply it to the next debt: Car 2. So here is what your overall debt picture will now look like:

Debt Name	Balance	Monthly Payment
Doctor	PAID	OFF! (Freed Up $200)
Credit Card 2	PAID	OFF! (Freed Up $100)
Credit Card 1	PAID	OFF! (Freed Up $150)
Car 2	$4,250	$850
Car 1	$5,200	$500
Student Loan	$12,250	$200
Total	$21,700	$1,550

DFD: 14 months

Do this for five months and BAM! – one of the car payments is gone! See how quickly this happens? Now your debt picture looks like this:

Debt Name	Balance	Monthly Payment
Doctor	PAID OFF!	(Freed Up $200)
Credit Card 2	PAID OFF!	(Freed Up $100)
Credit Card 1	PAID OFF!	(Freed Up $150)

Car 2	PAID OFF!	(Freed Up $400)
Car 1	$2,700	$500
Student Loan	$11,250	$200
Total	$13,950	$700

How exciting is this? You can see the light at the end of the tunnel! Now you only have two more debts left to pay off. Since we just freed up $850, the other car payment will be gone in a blink of an eye. Here is what that will look like:

Debt Name	Balance	Monthly Payment
Doctor	PAID	OFF! (Freed Up $200)
Credit Card 2	PAID	OFF! (Freed Up $100)
Credit Card 1	PAID	OFF! (Freed Up $150)
Car 2	PAID	OFF! (Freed Up $400)
Car 1	$2,700	$1,350
Student Loan	$11,250	$200
Total	$13,950	$1,550

DFD: 9 months

In two months, we won't have any car payments! Think how sweet it will feel to drive paid-in-full cars. Here is an updated look at our debt picture:

Debt Name	Balance	Monthly Payment
Doctor	PAID	OFF! (Freed Up $200)
Credit Card 2	PAID	OFF! (Freed Up $100)
Credit Card 1	PAID	OFF! (Freed Up $150)
Car 2	PAID	OFF! (Freed Up $400)
Car 1	PAID	OFF! (Freed Up $500)
Student Loan	$10,850	$1,550
Total	$10,850	$1,550

At this point, your sole debt will be the student loan. You can apply $1,550 a month towards this. Talk about a big snowball! Doing this for another seven months will lead to DEBT FREEDOM!

Let's take a minute to reflect. You started off with $52,700 in debt. Now, 34 months later, you are debt free! How amazing is that? What a great feeling this will be! No more late-night calls from collection agencies. You'll be able to peacefully shut your eyes at night. I told you that you can do this!

Unexpected Benefits of Being Debt-Free

You can probably make a list of the great things that will happen when you no longer have any non-house/non-business debt. There are also some other benefits of being debt-free you may not realize. Here are some of those:

A. You Will Sleep Better

I personally know some people who have a lot of debt. They do not sleep very well and they wake up numerous times during the night. I am sure that owing someone money contributes to their sleepless nights.

B. You Will Be Able to Give Money Away

It is great to be able to buy things and invest your money to have it grow, but being able to give money away might be the greatest reason to get out of debt. Imagine writing a $10,000 check to your church and it not bouncing! Think of one of the wealthiest people on Earth, Oprah Winfrey. She has made more money than you and I probably ever will. She can buy (and has probably bought) pretty much anything she wants. However, when she talks about what gives her great joy, it has nothing to do with anything she has bought for herself. One of Oprah's greatest joys is the school she started in South Africa. Material things come and go. Helping others can create a legacy that will last generations.

C. You Can Invest Like Never Before

When you are not paying someone else interest, you can use this money to earn interest for yourself by investing. This is known as compound interest. Compound interest can be thought of as earning interest on interest that has already been paid to you; we will discuss this in greater detail in the next chapter.

D. Your Spouse Will Be Happy

Tracy and I established our hopes and dreams (Kindergarten in The School of Financial Freedom) before we even got married. Because of this, we have always been on the same page when it comes to our finances. We have financial margin in place and this has strengthened our marriage in more ways than a savings account can show. With two daughters in various activities added to our teaching schedules, our lives can be pretty hectic. Because our mortgage is our only debt, we never argue about money. This enables us to focus on other things which makes our bond that much stronger.

E. Paid-For-in-Advance Vacations Are Amazing

Imagine having your summer vacation not follow you home in the form of credit card bills. I have paid for vacations using a credit card and for some upfront in cash. The ones I paid for with cash were much more relaxing and enjoyable than the ones I paid for using my credit card.

F. You Need to Earn Less to Maintain the Same Lifestyle

When you no longer are making debt payments, you get to keep that money instead. Therefore, you do not need to make as much to maintain your current lifestyle. For instance, let's say you need $3,000 a month to live and cover your expenses. Five hundred dollars of this is credit card debt payments. Once the debt is gone, you need only $2,500 to maintain the same lifestyle!

Once you are debt-free other than the mortgage, you can really start to have some fun. In the next chapter, we are going to talk about saving money for the long-term, so that your Golden Years can truly be Golden!

YOUR HOMEWORK

List your debts in order from least to greatest and begin paying off your smallest debt first and continue going in this order until you have eliminated all of your debt.

C H A P T E R   8

How Most Teachers Have a Head Start on Retirement

"The power of compound interest is the most powerful force in the universe."

ALBERT EINSTEIN

While most of us know how important it is to save for retirement, a majority of us are not doing a good job   with this. In fact, 52 percent of Americans have less than $10,000 saved for retirement.[a]

As scary as that is, I have an even scarier stat for you: 28 percent of Americans have less than $1,000 saved for retirement.[b]

The good news for you is that most of you (depending on the state you teach in) have a retirement account in the form of a teacher retirement system. More on that in a bit.

How Does This Happen?

I remember when I really first started thinking about retirement. Like most of you, when I first started teaching, I went to a new teacher orientation before the start of the school year. This is where I learned about all the benefits the district offered: health insurance, disability insurance, the retirement plan, etc. I remember listening to a few gentlemen explain the retirement plan and the importance of saving and thinking, "Really, I'm a teacher. I don't make enough to save for my retirement. I am worried about next week, not 30 years down the road." I then went home and thought about some people I knew.

There were some who had needed to continue working even though they wanted to retire because they had never properly prepared for retirement. No matter how much they were making, they convinced themselves that it was just never enough to invest in themselves. This held true when they were 24, 34, 44, and 54 years old. Now they found themselves with no choice but to have to continue working to support themselves.

At the same time, I also thought of someone else: my grandmother, Meno. Meno is someone who never made more than $50,000 a year, yet invested in herself, lived way below her means, and saved for retirement. She was able to retire at 59 and has the freedom to do what she wants. In fact, when Tracy, Ava, and I moved from Florida to Georgia, she was able to buy a house three doors down from us outright before selling her house in Florida! Now, on those cold Georgia days she has the freedom to be able to sit in her cozy living room with a fire going and not have to go to work. This was all because she made the decision to sacrifice immediate pleasures for long-term options.

I don't think anyone intentionally wants to retire with

barely anything in her account. We all work too hard and get up too early for 40 years to have nothing to show for it. Unfortunately, it happens pretty easily.

We start our teaching careers earning very little. We promise ourselves we will start investing in a couple years after we are making more money. However, we get used to every raise we get and our lifestyle follows our salary. So, we go along like this for 30 years, and when we want to step out of the classroom, we find ourselves with little saved. We are then faced with the fact that even though we have done our part and taught thousands of students, we don't have many options. Unfortunately, we quit but stay. That's right: mentally we check out but physically we have to continue working. I don't want that to be you. We need to change this!

What Is TRS

Most states offer their teachers a type of pension called the Teacher Retirement System. There are different formulas depending on the state you live in but, since I live in Georgia, I am going to use the Georgia TRS for my examples (to find out the specifics of your state, Google "the name of your state" and "teacher's retirement system"). The way it works in Georgia is that a teacher will get a monthly check in retirement if she is vested: that is, has worked for 10 years as a member of TRS. Classified employees (teachers, paraprofessionals, principals, etc.) are such members. Upon getting paid, this group of employees automatically has 6 percent taken out of their check and invested in TRS. They have no say in the decision.

They then are paid benefits in retirement based upon the number of years they have worked and their salary. The formula is pretty simple: a TRS member gets 2 percent per year of the highest salary he earned for 24 consecutive months. I know it sounds more complicated than it really is. Basically, take the average of the two highest paid years of employment. Then you multiply the number of years he has worked by 2 percent to determine the percentage he would receive. So let's put this in real-world numbers. We will say Jenny was a teacher for 30 years and the average salary of her two highest paid years was $60,000. So, we take the number of years worked (30) and multiply that by 2 percent to get 60 percent. We then take $60,000 and multiply it by 60 percent to get $36,000. That would be Jenny's annual pay-out (before cost-of-living increases) from the time she retires until she passes away. This is a great benefit that most other workers do not have!

If you work 30 years, you get this benefit right when you retire. So let's say you started teaching at age 23. You teach for 30 years and then call it a career. You will be 53 and will start collecting your TRS benefits the following month and will continue receiving these benefits until you die. So, using the numbers mentioned above, you would start collecting $36,000 a year beginning at age 53. Let's say you live until you are 93. You would have collected over $1.4 million! Not too bad.

As great as that sounds, I know many of you are thinking there is no way I am going to make it 30 years in the classroom. What does that mean for you? Well, as long as you have 10 years in the system, you are still eligible to receive this benefit. For example, let's assume you taught 15 years. We will say the average of your two highest paid years was $50,000. We take 15 (number of years taught) times 2 percent to get 30 percent. So you will get 30 percent of $50,000. This is $15,000 a year or $1,250 a month! Not too shabby. You won't be able to start collecting this until you turn 60, but just think: from then on, most of your monthly food bills will be taken care of.

Social Security

Now we all know how great the government is at handling money (sarcasm included) so they help us out a little with Social Security. There are many ways one can take Social Security. In fact, there are so many loopholes that entire books have been written about how to best utilize this. I am not even going to try and begin to explain all these ways but highly recommend a great book titled *Get What's Yours: The Secrets to Maxing out Your Social Security*, written by Laurence J. Kotlikoff, Philip Moeller, and Paul Solman. It goes through and explains all the different ways to utilize this program.

In addition, here is a great site you can visit to help you see the difference in the amount you will receive in Social Security depending on when you start collecting:

http://bit.ly/2ztB4YU

I don't want you to rely solely on Social Security for your money in retirement, but it can be a great resource for you. There are numerous ways you can take Social Security but the most important factor to consider is the age in which you begin drawing it.

For anyone born in 1960 or later, full retirement age is currently sixty-seven years old. Full retirement age is the age in which you will receive 100 percent of your full, calculated benefit. If you wait until this age to start collecting, it can benefit you greatly!

You can start collecting Social Security benefits at age 62. While this may sound tempting, the earlier you start collecting, the less money you will collect. If you start to receive Social Security benefits at 62, you will only receive 70 percent of your full, calculated benefits. If you waited until you were 64, you would receive 80 percent of your full benefit. At 65, you would receive 85 percent and at 66, you would get 93 percent. To better illustrate this, I just looked at my estimated Social Security benefits. If I started collecting at my full retirement age (67), my monthly payment would be about $1,862. If I waited until 70, my monthly payment would be about $2,331. If I started collecting at 62, my monthly payment would be about $1,263. To see what your Social Security benefits look like, visit www.ssa.gov/my statement and open an account.

The main thing to remember is that if you start collecting Social Security any time before you are 67, you will lose money and never get it back! If you decide to start collecting at age 62, you will get 70 percent of your benefit the rest of your life. It does not change when you turn 67.

I know this might be difficult, but if you hold off until age 70 to start receiving Social Security, you will get 124 percent of your full benefit! Pretty good deal if you can do it. The beauty is, most of you might be able to do this since you will have a pension.

Speaking of which, your pension might affect your Social Security benefits. There are some states in which teachers (and other public service employees) do not pay into Social Security. I don't want to confuse you too much with this so here is a resource that can help you understand a little more:

http://bit.ly/2AvAElh

I would also encourage you to talk with someone in HR and/or your financial advisor to learn more about your pension and social security and see how the combination affects you.

Supplemental Retirement Accounts;
What Are My Options?

As a school teacher, you have the option to potentially invest in a variety of retirement plans: 403(b)s, 457s, and possibly Roth 403(b)s and Roth 457s. I know some of these may be foreign and sound scary. Don't worry. Most of you have heard of a 401(k). The 403(b) plans are basically 401(k) plans for teachers. The number and lettering is used by the IRS for tax purposes and the types of plans listed here are for non-profit employers, such as school districts. The following is a listing and discussion about the various types of retirement plans.

403bs

You invest money into a 403(b) plan before you are taxed on it. This helps you get more bang for your buck upfront. Let's assume you are in the 25 percent tax bracket. If you invested $100 into a 403(b) plan, only $75 would be deducted from your paycheck! If you had kept the entire $100, you would be taxed on it immediately. If you were taxed 25 percent of this amount, your purchasing power (the amount you see in your paycheck) would only be $75. Remember, Uncle Sam always gets his money, so your 403(b) investment get taxed down the road when you withdraw it in retirement. However, this money *grows* tax-deferred until that time.

A big consideration when deciding if this is the correct option for you is anticipating when you will need to take this money out. There are some special considerations, but for the most part, this money cannot be touched without penalty until you turn 59 ½ years old.

457s

The 457 plan is pretty much a 403(b) with one huge difference: the money invested in it can be taken out before you reach age 59 ½ without having to pay a penalty. This can be attractive for school teachers because many retire before reaching that age.

Let's say you started teaching at age 23. You teach for 30 years and, thus, are able to start collecting your TRS benefits at age 53. As we discussed earlier, this will take care of 60 percent of your income (remember 30 years multiplied by 2 percent = 60 percent of the average of your two highest paid years). While many will not fully quit working entirely at age 53, some may want to. This is where the 457 plan can come into play. Once you separate from service, you can start collecting on this account.

A word of caution here: remember, your retirement savings need to get you through your living years. With the advances in medicine, many of us can expect to live well into our 80s and 90s. Your retirement savings need to be there then to help you live the life you envisioned. If you start taking money from your retirement account at age 53, it will probably not last as long as it would if you waited.

Roth 403(b)s and 457s

These plans are very similar to 403(b)s and 457s with one huge difference: the money is invested in these accounts after taxes are paid. We will use the $100 example mentioned above. If you invested $100 a month into a Roth 403(b) or 457, this money would be invested after you paid taxes on it. Therefore, the entire $100 would be deducted from your paycheck. However, since you are paying taxes on this money now, you will not be taxed on any of it (including the earnings you make) when you take distributions in retirement! So you are basically taking the hit now, rather than later.

What Is Best for Me?

I get asked this question quite often, and to get the best answer, you need to answer the following question: What will your tax bracket be when you retire? Tough one, huh? No one can really answer this question, as we have no clue. The way our government is racking up debt, many assume it will be higher in retirement than it is currently, but no one knows for sure. I don't really feel there is a right or wrong answer here: I am just happy you are saving! In fact, that is the most important thing to remember. Far too many people get caught up in the little details that become moot if you don't take the most important step and invest in yourself.

I Want More Information: Where Can I Look?

I have given a pretty general overview of these plans, but please ask your central office for more information on your supplemental retirement plan for more information. In addition, not all districts offer all of these types of plans. I just wanted to give you a basic overview before we begin.

I also want to let you know about a wonderful resource you have available to you. In 2000, Dan Otter was like most of you: a teacher. He became fed up with the lack of information that was given to teachers about their retirement plans. Some of you might even have felt his pain. This information was usually given to him through sales pitches at various school settings. In fact, he first learned about the 403(b) when a sales rep entered his classroom and tried to talk him into investing in a "TSA" which Dan later learned was a high-fee product (on the positive side, Dan did not enroll in this plan). Dan became so upset that he decided to do something to help teachers understand better their retirement options and created a free resource for us to visit: www.403bwise.com. In addition, he has also written a couple of books. I strongly encourage you to visit his site to get much more information about your retirement plans.

How Do You Get Started?

Most school districts have at least one vendor that handles their employees' retirement needs. This vendor could be a company like VALIC Financial Advisors, Lincoln Financial Group, or TIAA. There are many more but these are the companies I usually see when talking with teachers here in Georgia. This vendor has a local financial representative that will sit down and help you plan for your retirement. They will go over your options on what mutual funds to invest in. Many times you will be given a questionnaire to determine what type of investor you are. Some teachers are very conservative whereas others are willing to accept a lot of risk. Remember, the person who cares the most about your money and your future is the one who looks back at you each morning in the mirror.

During this meeting, you will discuss how much you are willing to invest every month. Once this is decided, your payroll person is notified and this amount is taken out of your paycheck each month before you have a chance to see it, get used to it, and, thus, spend it. This is a strategy known as dollar-cost averaging. Too many of us spend our entire paychecks (if not more). This is why it's so important to have this money taken out before you have a chance to get used to it as income. Using this approach, you are not trying to time the market. You are investing for the long haul and will use the magic of compound interest to build wealth; we will discuss this magic in a bit.

The beauty of having TRS is that you don't have to invest too much to ensure your standard of living remains the same when you retire. Many teachers already live off less than 100 percent of their salaries. When you take out your TRS contributions, healthcare and other deductions, you may find that you are actually living off 80 percent of your salary. If you teach 30 years, you will collect 60 percent of your salary in TRS (remember, that is the case here in Georgia and it may vary depending on where you live). Throw in a little Social Security and you don't have to invest too much each month to ensure your standard of living doesn't decline when you step out of the classroom.

I think it is a good idea to start by investing $100 a month (6th Grade in the School of Financial Freedom). Some districts ask that you designate the amount you are investing using percentages. If this is the case, get as close to $100 a month as possible. The beauty of this is, when you get a raise, the amount you are investing will automatically increase, too, without you having to do anything. Once you get to 9th Grade in The School of Financial Freedom, you will increase the amount you are investing to 15 percent. An advantage of investing in your school district's supplemental retirement account is that it can be adjusted at any time. With health insurance, you usually have an open enrollment period in which you make a decision that cannot be changed after this period ends; you are stuck for the coming year with the decision you made. With your supplemental retirement account, you can change the amount you are contributing at any time (once again, check with you central office to make sure this is the case in your district).

Remember, this account is to help you bridge the gap when you stop working. Since you have TRS you do not need to save as much as someone without this benefit to maintain the same lifestyle in retirement. However, we need this money to last us up to 40 years. With the advances in modern medicine, many of us will live into our 80s and even 90s. In fact, if you are a female and live to be 65, your odds of making it until you are 85 are greater than 50 percent.[c]

This is why it is so important to invest in yourself!

What Are Mutual Funds?

In most retirement plans, you will be investing in mutual funds. I am fairly confident that most of you have heard of these, but you may not know exactly what they are.

A mutual fund is an investment in which investors (like you) put their money together into one professionally managed investment. You are mutually funding this investment with others. Mutual funds can invest in stocks, bonds, cash, and/or other assets.

To make it a little easier, think of mutual funds as buckets of different investments. One bucket may hold stocks such as Apple and Coca-Cola. Another bucket may hold bonds. So, when you purchase a mutual fund you are purchasing a bucket of whatever type you selected. For example, let's say you bought shares of the Vanguard Value Index mutual fund. You may see this fund listed with the following symbol: VIVAX. Stocks use ticker symbols as an abbreviation so that you do not have to type in the entire name when looking it up. This mutual fund seeks to track the performance of a benchmark index that measures the investment return of large-capitalization value stocks. In simple terms, this fund is made up of individual stocks of large capital companies such as Microsoft, Exxon Mobil, Johnson & Johnson, GE, and AT&T. A great place to learn more about the holdings of a mutual fund is Yahoo Finance. Type in the ticker symbol of the mutual fund and you can learn much more information about it.

Here is another way to look at a mutual fund. Let's say the PE coach at your school decides to open a mutual fund but needs some people to help him. He asks some of your colleagues and they each agree to invest $50 in this fund. These teachers just mutually funded this investment. Since the PE coach opened this mutual fund, we will say he is the manager. The manager tells you what type of fund this is. For example, if he bought stock in large market capitalization companies it would be a Large Cap Fund. If he bought bonds, it would be a Bond Mutual Fund. I know the term mutual fund can sound intimidating, but it is not too hard to understand. Basically, mutual funds are formed when investors combine their money and invest in something together (mutually).

There are three big advantages that mutual funds offer: they are simpler to understand for the average person, they offer diversity, and they are accessible to most of us. Most of us do not have the time or knowledge to build our own retirement accounts composed of individual stocks and bonds. We have to write lesson plans, get the kids to soccer, cook dinner, etc. Buying shares of mutual funds enables us to own a professionally managed portfolio without having to have extensive knowledge about investing strategies.

Mutual funds offer us diversity. Instead of having to research and purchase individual stocks to make sure we are diversified, we can purchase shares of mutual funds and this is done for us. This is important because you do not want to put all your eggs into one basket. Some of you remember the name Enron. This was a huge energy company that employed almost 20,000 people. It was bankrupted in the early 2000s and, unfortunately, many of its employees had invested heavily in their stock. These investors lost billions of dollars.[d]

This is why diversification is important.

Finally, mutual funds are easily accessible to us. Some stock purchases require a lot of money. This is pretty extreme, but one share of Berkshire Hathaway will cost you over $200,000.[e]

Through your school district, most of you have the option to start purchasing mutual funds by investing a little each month.

It Sounds So Simple. Why Don't More People
Take Advantage of This?

Unfortunately, we live in a "if it bleeds, it leads" type of society. Newscasts almost always start with negative stories because this sensationalism usually keeps viewers tuned in. This holds true with our money, too.

Think about when gasoline approaches $4 a gallon. It is front page news on most newspapers and one of the leading stories on many newscasts. I actually just put gas in my car two days ago for $2.09 a gallon. Of course, gas prices are nowhere near the headlines. This can have a negative effect on our retirement accounts. It's well known that a lot of people lost huge sums of money in the most recent stock market crash. If you turned on any of the national news shows in late 2008 and early 2009, you would have thought the sky was falling. There were reports of people losing everything, but for most people this wasn't true. On October 9, 2007, the Dow Jones Industrial Average closed at a then all-time high of 14,164. Fast forward to March 9, 2009: the Dow closed at 6,547. A huge loss for sure, but people didn't lose all their money. Some lost over half but not all.

While many were saying to get out of stocks and mutual funds at this time, I was actually okay with them dropping in value. In my opinion, money invested in stocks and mutual funds should stay invested for the long haul: at least 10 years. I am no financial genius and cannot predict how the market will perform in the future but I look at the past and feel okay.

Why Dollar Cost Averaging Works Well

Dollar cost averaging is the way I recommend you save for retirement. Remember, when you use this strategy, you are investing a set amount for retirement every month. You are not trying to time the market; you are buying mutual funds when the market is up and when the market is down.

You may have heard of terms bear market and bull market. A bear market is one in which the stock market is in a downturn whereas a bull is when the market is going up. Many people get scared when we are in a bull market but it can actually be a good thing for your retirement account when you are thinking long-term and using the dollar cost average strategy. Let's see what I mean.

Dave Ramsey's team tracked the values of an S&P 500 index mutual fund for one year starting in September 2008 (this was the month the market started a free fall). They wanted to see what it looked like if you invested $500 in this fund on the first business day of each month for one year. As the value of this fund dropped, your $500 monthly investment bought more shares. To show this, let's say the fund was worth $20 in September 2008. Your $500 would have bought 25 shares ($500 divided by $20 equals 25). What if the fund dropped to $10 a share by March 2009? Well, you would have bought 50 shares that month ($500 divided by $10 equals 50). Ramsey's team found that by the end of that 12-month period, you would have ended up with a total of 440 shares with the average price per share coming in at less than $14. Since then, these 440 shares have grown in value. You paid a total of $6,000 for them ($500/month times 12 months) but now they are worth $34 per share. That totals $14,960![f]

Here is another example of why dollar cost averaging works so well. We will say you received an income tax refund of $2,400. You want to use this to invest in your favorite fund. You could invest this entire amount in one fell swoop. However, what if that was the exact day it hit an all-time high of $100 per share? Then you would have purchased 24 shares; $100/share multiplied by 24 shares = $2,400. Let's say the very next day the price dropped to $90/share. Your $2,400 would now be worth only $2,160. I bet you would not be feeling very good at this point.

What if you decided instead to dollar cost average this and bought $400 of this fund every month for six months ($400/month multiplied by 6 = $2,400)? The price of this fund could (and probably would) rise and fall each month. This means you would be purchasing different amounts each month. Let's say it looked like this each month:

Month 1 - $100 per share = 4 shares
Month 2 - $80 per share = 5 shares
Month 3 - $50 per share = 8 shares
Month 4 - $40 per share = 10 shares
Month 5 - $80 per share = 5 shares
Month 6 - $100 per share = 4 shares

I know this fund fluctuated a lot but wanted you to see the benefits of investing using the dollar cost averaging approach. Instead of purchasing 24 shares you would have purchased 36 shares. The average price would have been about $66.66 ($2,400/36 shares = $66.66). This is a lot better than $100/share it would have cost if you invested the entire $2,400 at once. For the same $2,400 investment, you would have been able to purchase 12 more shares!

Using the dollar cost averaging strategy minimizes the impact of your losses when the market drops. Mutual funds and stocks are the one thing most of us don't like to buy on sale. However, keeping your eyes on the long run and recognizing when we are in a bear market, allows you to increase how much you will have in retirement at a reduced cost. Remember, many of us get into trouble with our finances because of behavior and emotions. Dollar cost averaging can help with this. I know this may sound a little confusing but if you invest in the retirement plan offered by your school district you will be using this strategy! You can do this.

What Is the S&P 500 and the Dow?

Many of you have probably heard others refer to the Dow and the S&P 500 when discussing stocks and mutual funds. So what exactly are both of these? The Dow refers to the Dow Jones Industrial Average (DJIA). It is a stock market index that shows how 30 large publicly owned companies based in the United States have traded during a standard trading session in the stock market. It is often used to measure the United States industry. The S&P 500 (the Standard and Poor's 500 Index) is an index of 500 stocks chosen for market size, liquidity, and industry grouping, among other factors. The S&P 500 is designed to be a leading indicator of U.S. stocks. Basically, these two stock indexes provide a basis for how strong the U. S. stock market is.

If you judge stocks by these two indexes, they have done pretty well over the course of time. The Dow averaged almost 8% annual growth from 1921 to 2016.[g] The S&P 500 averaged 9.8% annual growth from 1928 to 2016.[h]

Now that is not saying that stocks grow this amount every year; rather, it is their average. Some years the market is up 15 percent and other years it is down 20 percent; however, the average growth over this period was between almost 8 to 9.8 percent. This time frame encompassed two World Wars, the Great Depression, and the tragedy of 9/11. Based on this past performance, I feel okay investing in mutual funds. I am not guaranteed any growth at all, but since I look at past performance as my guide, I don't get too freaked out when the market dips. Let's say you see a sweater at Macy's that costs $50. This is too much for you so you choose not to buy it. Two weeks later it goes on sale for half off. At this price, you might consider buying it. That is the way I view the stock market. When it's down, I look at it like I'm buying stocks and mutual funds on sale.

Have a Mental Picture of What Your Retirement Will Look Like

When Tracy and I moved to Georgia, I had just one request: a new television set. Shortly before moving, the new high-definition sets came out. I remember watching my first football game in high-def. It was amazing! The action was so vivid and the picture was so clear. When it comes to saving for your retirement, I want you to create a mental image as clear as one on the highest-definition television sets you can find. This is such a key to maintain the discipline to save month after month and year after year. You have to have a clear picture to help keep you going.

In most marriages, there is usually someone who is more of a free spirit and the other one is more of the nerd; in my case, I am the nerd. I love doing calculations and figuring how much money we will have saved at different increments in our lives. While Tracy is somewhat interested when I discuss this, she doesn't get as excited as I do. I needed to create a mental image for her. I found the most beautiful picture of a beach. This helped her get more excited than a spreadsheet full of numbers did. You see, that is what we are saving for: freedom. In fact, our retirement account could be renamed our freedom fund. This is the money that will help you pursue your passions later in life.

Even though I am a numbers guy, I occasionally still need some visuals to help me stay on track. I mentioned earlier how we surprised Ava and Ella with a trip to Disney World. I have to admit, there are times I get tunnel vision and focus too much on what I have going on and not enough on the present. When we went to Disney, I pretty much put my phone away and focused exclusively on my family. It was one of the greatest moments in my life. I had so much fun with them and we created memories that will last us forever. In my retirement, I want to relive that experience with grandchildren I don't have yet. Heck, I want to take them so many times that Mickey and Minnie will know their names. So, anytime I am tempted to spend money, I look at a picture of my family. This helps me stay the course. Without this reminder, it would be pretty easy to buy something today instead of investing for tomorrow. I would even be justified in doing so. When I left teaching in 2014, I had jobs that required me to drive a lot! Even when I was not driving out of town and just reporting to the office, my round-trip commute was 82-miles (before this, my round trip to school and home was 6 miles). I put over 20,000 miles on my car in one year! I could have easily convinced myself to trade in my 2002 SUV for something more modern. My vehicle is so old that I can't even plug in my I-Phone because I-Phones weren't around when it was designed! However, I need only one look at this picture and I know I'm making the correct decision in driving it as long as it runs. Without that visual, it would be much easier to treat myself today rather than save for my future.

How Much Does It Cost To Save?

Here is where the fun begins. I recommend you try to start by saving at least $100 a month for retirement (6th Grade in The School of Financial Freedom). However, this might be a little too much at first for you. If that is the case, I want you to start somewhere. Let's say you just begin by investing 1 percent of your salary. What does that look like?

If your annual salary is $32,000, 1 percent a month would be $26.66. However, if you invested this in a 403(b) or 457, only about $21.33 would be deducted from your check. Remember, money invested these types of accounts are deducted before taxes are withheld. If you kept the entire $26.66 and were taxed on it, you'd only have around $21.33 more in your check. If your annual salary is $50,000, 1 percent a month would be $41.67, but your check would be only approximately $31.25 less. I know this doesn't seem like much (around $1 a day) but let's see how it grows over time. If you invested $41.67 a month for 30 years and averaged 8 percent growth on the fund per year, you would have over $62,000 in your retirement account! That for a measly buck a day.

The Magic of Compound Interest

How in the world does that happen? Well, it results from a wonderful concept known as compound interest. I am not the brightest person so I make sure I pay attention to those much smarter than I. Albert Einstein is one such person and it is rumored that he said the following:

The power of compound interest is the most powerful force in the universe.

If Einstein says it, I am all ears. Compound interest is defined as interest which is calculated not only on the initial principal but also the accumulated interest of prior periods. I know, it sounds confusing, but basically you get paid interest on interest that has already been paid to you.

Before I show you how compound interest works, I want to tell you about something referred to as the "Rule of 72." This rule is a quick way to see how quickly the money you invest will double in value. The way to determine this is to take the number 72 and divide it by the percentage of interest you are earning. For example, if you earn an average of 5 percent a year on your investments, they will double in 14.4 years (72 divided by 5 equals 14.4). If you earn an average of 10 percent a year, they will double in 7.2 years (72 divided by 10 equals 7.2). To illustrate this a little more, we are going to pretend you invest $100 and this $100 grows at an average annual rate of 9 percent. Using the Rule of 72, this $100 will be $200 in 8 years (remember, 72 divided by 9 equals 8).

Here's an easy way to see the magic of compound interest. Let's say you invest $1,000 and this investment averages a 10 percent return a year. Because of compound interest, this money will double in a little over 7 years. The chart below shows you how this works.

Year	Money Earned from Interest	Total Amount of Money
0	$0.00	$1,000.00
1	$100.00 (10 percent of $1,000.00)	$1,110.00
2	$110.00 (10 percent of $1,110.00)	$1,210.00
3	$121.00 (10 percent of $1,210.00)	$1,331.00
4	$133.00 (10 percent of $1,331.00)	$1,464.00
5	$146.00 (10 percent of $1,464.00)	$1,610.00
6	$161.00 (10 percent of $1,610.00)	$1,771.00
7	$177.10 (10 percent of $1771.00)	$1,948.10

Just think, your initial $1,000 investment has almost doubled after seven years and you did not have to do anything except let it sit and grow! So, if you kept going with this, after 14 years you would have almost $4,000. After 21 years, almost $8,000. After 28 years, almost $16,000! All from a $1,000 investment. That is why Einstein said compound interest is so powerful!

Let's take a look at a couple more examples. We will say that you start investing shortly after you begin teaching at age 25. You invest $100 a month in a 403(b) supplemental retirement account. We will be conservative and say you average 6 percent growth on this each year. After 10 years, you will have a little over $16,000. You are now 35 and are still able to continue investing $100 a month. You do this for another 10 years. You are now 45 and have a little over $45,000 in your account. Life is starting to get a little hectic and you have more expenses but still are disciplined and continue investing $100 a month for 10 more years. You are now 55 and have a little over $97,000 in your account. You figure you will work another ten years (maybe not in teaching but another field or part-time since you will now have your teacher retirement money coming in) and don't want to start taking distributions until you are 65. The kids are going to college and mom and dad had to move in with you. You just can't afford to invest $100 each month so you stop contributing. However, you leave this $97,000 in your account and it continues to grow at 6 percent a year. Ten years go by and guess how much you now have. Over $174,000! Yes, you read that correctly. But wait, it gets a little better. We said you were investing $100/month in a 403(b). Remember, this is money taken out before taxes so your paycheck was only reduced by about $75/month. This is a little above $2.50 a day. So basically, for the price of a Diet Coke from a vending machine a day, you would have almost $175,000! You could buy your very own vending machine with that amount.

Here is another example. Let's say you are 25 and decide to buy a brand new car (on a side note, I almost always recommend buying a reliable used car since you get hit big time with depreciation when buying new). The average price of a brand new car is $33,650.[i]

We will say your monthly car payment is $600. Now, you really want to pay this off as fast as possible so you decide to add $400 a month to your payment and are, thus, paying $1,000 each month on this car note. Fast-forward three years and this payment is gone! Now, here is the key: we are not going to blow this $1,000. We are going to continue making monthly payments, but to ourselves. For two years, pay yourself $1,000 every month and put it into your savings account. You are now 30 years old, have a paid-for car and $24,000 in your savings account. Now, when this car needs to be replaced years down the road, you will be able to use this $24,000 and buy another car outright!

We are now going to continue paying ourselves first for another five years. You are already used to living without this $1,000, so now we are going to invest this amount each month. In case you were wondering, in 2018 you can invest up to $18,500 a year in your 403(b) plan (if you are 50 or older, you can invest an additional $6,000 a year in this plan for a grand total of $24,500 a year). We are going to assume you average 6 percent growth per year on this. You stop investing at age 35 with over $69,000 in your retirement account. Now, you do whatever you want with this $1,000 a month, but don't touch your retirement account for 30 years.

This $69,000 continues to grow at 6 percent a year until you hit 65. Guess how much it would be worth then? Drum roll please ... almost $400,000! WOW! By paying yourself an amount that is a little over a car payment for five years you could pretty much be set in retirement. See, I told you that you can do this.

In fact, let's say your parents invested $1,000 when you were born and it grew at 10 percent per year. When you turn 65, guess how much it would be worth? Over $490,000! Pretty powerful, huh?

Here is a final way to see how compound interest works. If I asked you would you rather have $1,000 right now or a penny that doubles in value every day for one month which would you select? I am sure you probably have guessed that there is a catch and would select the penny but to show you how right you are, this penny would be worth over $5 million after 30 days. Here's how:

Day	Amount
1	$0.01
2	$0.02
3	$0.04
4	$0.08
5	$0.16
6	$0.32
7	$0.64
8	$1.28
9	$2.56
10	$5.12
11	$10.24
12	$20.48
13	$40.96
14	$81.92
15	$163.84
16	$327.68
17	$655.36
18	$1,310.72
19	$2,621.44
20	$5,242.88
21	$10,485.76
22	$20,971.52
23	$41,943.04
24	$83,886.08
25	$167,772.16
26	$335,544.32
27	$671,088.64
28	$1,342,177.28
29	$2,684,354.56
30	$5,368,709.12

This is definitely an extreme example, but is meant to show you how fast something can compound. In addition to the quote I shared earlier, Einstein had another opinion concerning compound interest. Rumor has it that he said the following:

Compound interest is the eighth wonder of the world.
He who understands it, earns it ...
he who doesn't ... pays it.

It is pretty difficult to disagree with the man often referred to as the father of modern physics.

I have had the honor of meeting with thousands of school employees and helping them manage their money better and invest for their retirements. I would say the number one question I get at these events goes something like this, "Danny, I heard you talk about the magic of compound interest but I am still unsure. I can only save a little each month. Can it really grow into an amount that will help me when I stop working?" The answer is yes, it can! Even if you are not able to save a lot each month, start! Remember, small seeds grow into big trees.

YOUR HOMEWORK

Determine what your TRS (Teacher Retirement System) account will look like and find out what your benefit will be.

Come up with an estimate on what your Social Security payments will look like; this website can help:

https://www.ssa.gov/retire/estimator.html

Talk with someone at the central office to learn more about the supplemental retirement plans offered in your district and how to get started investing.

Create a mental image of how you want your retirement to look.

CHAPTER 9

No, You Do Not Have to Have a Mortgage Payment Forever

"Bad debt is debt that makes you poorer.
I count the mortgage on my home as bad debt,
because I'm the one paying on it."

ROBERT KIYOSAKI

Before we discuss the mortgage, let's take a minute to revisit The School of Financial Freedom. Here are the grade levels:

Kindergarten	Know Your Why/Set Goals
1st Grade	Get Health, Automobile, and Homeowner's/Renter's Insurance
2nd Grade	Get Disability Insurance
3rd Grade	Get Life Insurance
4th Grade	Get a Will
5th Grade	Save One Month of Expenses
6th Grade	Invest $100/Month for Retirement

7th Grade	Eliminate All Debt Except the Mortgage
8th Grade	Save at Least Three Months of Expenses
9th Grade	Invest 15 percent of Your Salary for Long-Term Dreams
10th Grade	Pay off Your Mortgage
11th Grade	Invest 30percent of Your Salary for Long-Term Dreams
12th Grade	Do Whatever You Want and Live a Prosperous Life

We start focusing on paying off the mortgage in 10th grade. If you are in this grade, you have at least three months of expenses saved, are investing 15 percent of your salary for retirement, and have no debt except your mortgage. Now we can start attacking that last debt: your mortgage! In fact, this might not take as long as you think.

Let's use the numbers from Chapter 7. You started off with $52,700 in total debt and were paying $1,550/month towards this debt. Once that debt was eliminated, you used this $1,550 to build your savings to cover at least three months of expenses (8th Grade in The School of Financial Freedom). After this is done, you can use a portion of the $1,550 to invest 15 percent of your salary and use the remaining to pay off your mortgage. This can happen sooner than you ever imagined.

Buying a House: The Mortgage

For most of us, a mortgage will be the largest debt we carry in our lives. Purchasing a house makes financial sense for a number of reasons. Over a good period of time, real estate and home values normally appreciate. However, like investing in the stock market, this increase is not a given every year.

If you plan on living somewhere for a short period of time (less than five years), it might make more sense to rent so that you will not have to worry about selling your house when it is time to move. A second advantage of owning a home is, once you pay it off, you will have a place to live rent-free for the remainder of your time in that house. In addition, if you do decide to sell and move somewhere else, you will have equity in this house and, generally speaking, make tax-free money from this sale.

To briefly illustrate this, suppose a person decides to rent rather than purchase a home. Their rent is $750/month. This adds up to a total of $9,000 a year spent on housing. The person lives there for ten years and then decides to move. They will have paid $90,000 in rent with nothing to show for it. Suppose this person purchased a house instead for $125,000, put 20 percent down and took out a 15-year loan with a 4 percent interest rate. Using these terms, their mortgage would be $100,000. This would leave them with the same monthly payment (about $750 not including taxes and insurance) as the rent. After ten years they decide to move. If the house had increased in value by 1 percent each year, it would be valued at $138,077 after ten years. Because he had been making monthly payments on this debt, he now owes only $40,164 on this loan. Even with a real estate selling charge of 6 percent, he would walk away with $89,628!

An argument I have heard against owning a home is that it would be wiser to rent an inexpensive house and save the money that you would have spent on an expensive mortgage payment. It is hard to argue with the math. If one could rent a home for $500 a month instead of paying a mortgage payment of $1,000, it would free up $500 a month. This money could be used to build up the emergency fund or invest. While the math is clear, do you know many people who would actually save or invest ALL of this extra money? Even with the best intentions, something always seems to come up, and we find ways to spend this "extra" money. In the long-run, most people would spend this money on something that would be long gone after a few months.

According to the Bureau of Labor Statistics' Consumer Expenditure Survey, housing accounted for roughly one-third of American households' spending in 2015.[a]

Many realtors suggest that one can spend one-third of his/her gross pay on housing. That does hold true for many that are in the low-moderate income bracket. There are many that gross around $50,000 a year and search for homes in the $150,000 range. However, this logic seems to break down as we make more money. There are some who make $100,000 a year yet search for $400,000 homes. It seems as we earn more, we spend a greater percentage of our gross pay on our home. This limits one's options in life. Some choose to live so large that they have no money left over to take vacations, go out to eat, or even furnish their home. I point this out in case you fall into that category. If so, downsizing can be a great way to boost your financial situation.

Lose the Mortgage

Now that we have discussed the reasons people have mortgages, we are going to look at ways to get rid of this large debt. This is where the fun really begins! Look around your home, in your garage, and out your back door. Imagine the feeling of owning it all, free and clear. How would you feel?

Many people assume they will always have a house payment and don't realize how much interest they are paying on their loans. Let's say you buy a house for $150,000. You make a down payment of $30,000 and take out a 30-year mortgage for $120,000 with a 5 percent interest rate. If you made the regular monthly payment, your $150,000 house will have cost you $261,840 when all is said and done!

Here are a few ways you can pay off your mortgage faster:

1. Pay Extra

You can sign up for a 30-year loan and promise yourself that you will pay extra each month towards this loan. If you are serious about paying your home off early, this is probably not the best option. Most of us make promises we cannot keep. We might have the best intentions to pay extra each month but then something comes up: Valentine's Day in February, summer vacation in July, Christmas in December, and we find we need this "extra" money for something other than the house.

2. Make Biweekly Payments

If you do have a 30-year loan, you could sign up to make biweekly payments instead of a monthly payment. These biweekly payments will be half of your monthly payment but you will actually make an extra payment each year. Here is how this works. Let's say your monthly payment is $1,000. You would pay $12,000 each year towards your mortgage: 12 (months in a year) multiplied by $1,000 (monthly payment) = $12,000. If you used the biweekly approach, you'll pay $500 (half of the monthly $1,000 payment) every two weeks. There are 52 weeks in a year so you'll make 26 half payments. Multiplying $500 by 26 equals $13,000; thus, you will make one extra $1,000 payment each year. This can trim anywhere from five to seven years off your 30-year loan, depending on your interest rate. One warning about this approach: be careful that your mortgage company doesn't charge a fee for this. Some of them try to slip this in, so just make sure yours does not.

3. Refinance

Perhaps the easiest way to pay off your loan is to refinance. As I write this, interest rates are still historically low. My family moved from Florida to Georgia in the summer of 2006. We selected a 30-year loan. When interest rates dropped to record lows in 2013, we refinanced. We were able to lower our rate by three full points and reduced our term to ten years. We pay around $275 more each month compared to our original loan but will own our house free and clear much earlier and save almost $75,000 in interest! In addition, once this is paid off, we can pay **ourselves** a mortgage payment rather than our bank!

In fact, if all you did was simply lower your interest rate by 1 percent on a 30-year, $100,000 mortgage, you would save over $600 per year! You could apply this savings to your principal and pay off your mortgage a lot sooner.

Arguments Against Paying off Your Mortgage

There are some who argue against paying off the mortgage. Here are a few common arguments:

1. You Will Lose the Deduction on Your Taxes

One argument I have heard against paying off your mortgage early is that you won't be able to take the home mortgage interest deduction and reduce your taxable income. First, in order to claim this credit, you must itemize your deductions. Most Americans take the standard deduction so this wouldn't even matter to them.[b]

Let's pretend that you are not in the majority and itemize your deductions. As a teacher you are most likely in the 25 percent income tax bracket. Suppose you have a 30-year, $200,000 mortgage with a 5 percent interest rate. In the first year, you would pay approximately $10,000 in interest (5 percent of $200,000 is $10,000). Now for your big tax write-off. Your taxable income will lower by $10,000. Since you're in the 25 percent tax bracket, this deduction will lower the amount you owe in taxes by $2,500 (25 percent of $10,000 equals $2,500). So, if you think you should keep your mortgage because of this deduction, you are basically saying you should pay $10,000 a year in interest to your mortgage company so that you can reduce the amount you owe Uncle Sam by $2,500. Now I am not a mathematical genius, but paying $10,000 to save $2,500 doesn't make much sense to me. If this sounds good to you, please send me your contact information, and I will gladly write you a check for $2,500 in exchange for $10,000!

2. You Should Invest the Extra Money Instead of Paying It Towards the Mortgage

Another argument I have heard against paying off a mortgage early is that one could invest this money and earn more in the stock market. That is hard to argue against because, historically speaking, it is accurate. If your mortgage rate is 5 percent and you pay it off early you will, in essence, be earning 5 percent a year since you will no longer be paying a lender 5 percent; this money will remain in your bank account. The stock market has historically averaged more than 5 percent annual growth so paying extra towards your mortgage instead of investing this amount seems unwise. Here is where we have to look at the bigger picture.

If this is the case, why don't more people take out a home equity loan and invest it in the stock market? One could borrow money at a 5 percent set interest rate and earn more on this same money by investing it; sounds like a no-brainer to me. However, most people will not do this because they don't view their house as just an investment—

it is a huge part of who they are. In fact, according to a poll conducted by Allstate/The National Journal Heartland Monitor, the best reasons for home ownership are:

Having a place to raise a family	40 percent
Building equity rather than paying rent	26 percent
Making a good long-term investment	13 percent
Acquiring an asset you can pass along	9 percent
Being part of a neighborhood and community	6 percent
Following in your parents' footsteps	2 percent
Getting a tax deduction	2 percent[c]

While you could invest this money, imagine the feeling of owning all of your possessions! The grass in your backyard feels a lot different when you own it.

Let's Do the Math

To show you how this looks with real numbers, let's use the before-mentioned numbers using two different loan terms: a 30-year and a 15-year mortgage.

30-Year Mortgage

You recently purchased a $150,000 house and put 20 percent ($30,000) down on it. You then took out a 30-year, 5 percent interest rate loan for $120,000. Your monthly payment (excluding taxes and insurance) would be $644.19. This would total $7,730.28 a year. Multiply this by 30 years and you would get a grand total of $231,908.40. Add the $30,000 you used as your down payment and the total amount you will have paid on that $150,000 house will be $261,908.40. I bet you didn't hear that from the mortgage company! Let's see how we can pay the house off a lot faster.

Once again, we will use the numbers from Chapter 7.

After eliminating your debt, you had $1,550 freed up. You then used this money to build up your savings and then moved to 9th grade in The School of Financial Freedom: invest 15 percent of your salary for long-term dreams. We will say the amount invested was $625. That leaves $925 per month remaining. Let's apply this to the mortgage.

By adding $925 to your monthly mortgage payment of $644.19 and applying it to the principal, you will pay off your mortgage in 7 years, 7 months and save over $87,000 in interest! Now let's try this approach with a shorter-term mortgage.

15-Year Mortgage

When it comes to purchasing a house, I strongly encourage you to consider a 15-year loan. The monthly payments will be higher, but you will own your home outright in half the time compared to a 30-year loan. This frees up a huge amount of money to invest 30 percent of your income and do whatever you want.

Let's use the same numbers. Instead of a 30-year loan, you took out a 15-year, 4.5 percent interest rate loan for $120,000. Notice, the interest rate is lower than the one with the 30-year loan because, by taking on a shorter-term loan, you are usually able to get a better rate.

Your monthly payment (excluding taxes and insurance) would be $917.99. This would total $11,015.88 a year. Multiply this by 15 years and it equals $165,238.20. Add the $30,000 you used as your down payment and the total amount you will have paid on the $150,000 house will be $195,238.20! So let's pause a minute and think about this. Obtaining a 15-year mortgage instead of a 30-year will save you over $66,000 in interest when all is said and done. Yes, you will be paying a little over $273 more each month, but you will own the house completely 15 years sooner and save a lot of money.

It gets even better. Add the same $925 freed up from debt to your monthly payment. This makes your monthly payment $1,842.99/month. Doing this will enable you to pay off your mortgage in just 6 years, 9 months! In addition, the total amount you will have paid on that $150,000 house would only be $179,282. Can you imagine? In less than seven years, you will own your house outright!

Almost Sounds Too Good To Be True

Let's take a look to see how you have changed your life. You entered The School of Financial Freedom a little over 9 years ago. You had no goals, did not have disability or life insurance, had nothing in savings, were not saving anything in retirement, had $52,700 in debt and owed $120,000 on your mortgage.

You now have no debt; up are investing 15 percent of your salary; you have at least three months of expenses in your savings account; and you have a paid-off mortgage. Wow! Think about your future now. How bright will it be?

You will now be in 11th Grade in The School of Financial Freedom: Invest 30 percent of Your Salary for Long-Term Dreams. I bet if someone had told you a few years ago that you would be in the position to invest 30 percent of your salary, you would have thought they were talking about someone else. But here you are. In fact, you could easily invest more than 30 percent and not even really feel it!

Using the aforementioned numbers, we are assuming you make $50,000 a year. You started investing 15 percent of your income in 9th Grade, so we need to invest another 15 percent of your salary to get to 30 percent. To do this, we would need to invest an additional $625 a month.

We will say you had the 15-year mortgage just discussed. After paying off your debt and building your savings, you were paying $1,842.99 on your mortgage every month. After the mortgage is gone, you could invest an additional $625 every month and still have $1,200 left over! If you were investing 30 percent of a $50,000 annual salary, that would equate to $1,250 every month. To put an age on it, let's say you started doing this amount at age 40. Remember, you have already been investing 15 percent of your salary for a few years and your retirement account is worth $40,000 when you start investing $1,250 each month.

If you had $40,000 in your retirement account, invested $1,250 every month starting at age 40, averaged 8 percent growth per year on this and did this for 25 years, how much do you think you would have? If you guessed over $1.4 million, you are the winner! Talk about being able to do pretty much whatever you want. See, you can do this!

YOUR HOMEWORK

Look into refinancing your mortgage to see if you can get a lower interest rate. In addition, see if it would make sense to possibly decrease the number of years you have remaining on this loan by paying more each month.

CHAPTER 10

Other Important Parts of a Teacher's Financial Plan

"Teaching kids to count is fine, but teaching them what counts is best."

BOB TALBERT

Protect Yourself In The Classroom

In first through fourth grades you obtained insurance to protect yourself and you wrote a will to help your loved ones when you pass. I now want to cover another type of protection you should obtain to protect yourself in the classroom.

I am not always a big fan of unions because they can sometimes protect teachers that, quite frankly, probably shouldn't be in the classroom. Most teachers are wonderful but, like with any profession, there are a few bad apples. Unfortunately, these are the educators that the media usually like to focus on.[a]

This reminds me of when I was teaching kindergarten. It was my third year in the classroom so I was pretty low on the salary scale. There was a teacher down the hall from me that had been teaching much longer than I. Every afternoon during my planning break, I would pass her room and see her students there, plopped on the floor watching a video. I always thought to myself, "I could be teaching my students the most amazing lessons in the history of man. In fact, they could have grown five grade levels this year, but that teacher would still get paid more than I did." That is the crummy part of being a teacher: you definitely are not paid on job performance. I remember asking around as to why she was still in the classroom. It turns out my principal did try to get rid of her but faced some pressure from the local union, so this teacher was able to keep her job. That is why teacher unions get a bad rap.

On the flip side, they do a great job of protecting you, and this is why I strongly urge you to become a member. In this day and age of some people blaming teachers for all of society's ills, it is extremely important to have someone who has your back before you step foot into a classroom. Unfortunately, there are some parents who always take their child's side and this could come back to haunt you if you have no protection. A few years ago, I was teaching a special needs class in which most of my students had IQs below 30 and most did not verbally communicate. One day, one of the students came in with a huge black and blue bruise on his shoulder. It was the size of a brick. Since he could not explain to me what happened, I wrote a note home asking about this. He had been in my class for five years and I knew the family very well and felt confident that they would never hurt him; but, as you know, I had to inquire or I could get into legal trouble. The parents did not respond to my inquiry so I had no choice but to let the school counselor know. She was very concerned about the size of the bruise, so by law had to call the Department of Children and Family Services. They opened up an investigation and the parents became very upset with me. In fact, at Christmas they bought and delivered presents for everyone in the class (I had 4 para-professionals working with me) except for me. Even though I did the correct thing and was legally required to do so, I now had a family that did not like me. I was really glad that I was a member of an organization that offered me protection in case these parents made a crazy claim and tried to sue me. In Georgia this organization is called PAGE.

PAGE stands for The Professional Association of Georgia Educators. Members have easy access to attorneys, which are just a phone call away. Their professional liability coverage to protect a teacher's financial well-being in the event the teacher was sued by a parent or student includes the following:

- $1,000,000 per insured, per occurrence
- $3,000,000 per occurrence
- $3,000,000 aggregate per insured, per policy contract period
- $5,000 in bail bond availability for work-related criminal charges
- $2,500 Assault Related Personal Property Damage Endorsement

Their legal defense plan includes:

- Free access to PAGE Staff Attorneys
- $10,000 in Employment, certification and work-related criminal defense to protect your career ... *with no upfront costs (annual aggregate $20,000)!*

In addition to this legal protection, PAGE also works to improve teacher pay, benefits and working conditions; keeps educators informed on the key issues being discussed at the state level; and offers professional development opportunities. All of this for the relatively low price of $175 a year (beginning teachers pay only $87.50 for their first year of coverage). You get all of this for under $15 a month! In the type of society we now live in, I don't think any teacher should enter the classroom without this protection.

In case you want to know more about PAGE, please visit the following site: http://www.pageinc.org/?06

Never Cosign a Loan

Cosigning a loan for someone can completely derail your financial progress. Never, ever do this, not even for your own children! When you cosign a loan, you are responsible for it even though you may not even own it. In fact, if the loan is not paid, guess who might even get the first phone call: YOU! The creditors know that you are the person who has the money to actually pay for this. I know it can be hard to say no to a loved one, but do not put yourself in this position.

Focus on Net Worth

Many don't think too much about their net worth, but this shows your true financial standing. You determine your net worth by subtracting your liabilities (what you owe) from your assets (what you own). For example let's say you had the following assets:

House - $150,000 (this is what you reasonably expect it would sell it for)
Car - $10,000
Savings Account - $5,000
Retirement Account - $20,000

We will then say that you have the following liabilities (what you owe):

House - $75,000 (this what you still owe on your mortgage loan)
Car - $5,000

Student Loan - $20,000
Credit Cards - $5,000

Now we add up our assets and get a total of $185,000. We then subtract the total of our liabilities ($105,000) from our asset total and our net worth would be $80,000! When you focus on your net worth you are understanding that it is not what you have that counts, but rather what you own that determines your level of financial freedom.

In addition, focusing on net worth makes you look at things at little differently. For instance, I am not always happy about paying my mortgage. I know I need to but sometimes I think of the many other ways I could use this money. However, every month when I make a payment, I am increasing my net worth. Knowing this makes me look at making this payment a little differently.

The Legacy File

The Legacy File is something I got from Dave Ramsey's book *The Legacy Journey: A Radical View of Biblical Wealth and Generosity*. This file basically contains all of our family's important documents in one large envelope. This ensures we can find all of this information at a moment's notice. I talk to Tracy all the time about our finances, but she doesn't always remember what I said. This file is great for us. If something were to happen to me, she could look in one place and have all of this information. In addition, if we had to evacuate (we have had to before because of a tornado warning), we can just grab this file, bring it with us, and we will have all the information we need if we had to start over. I know it doesn't sound very optimistic, but it actually helps us sleep more soundly.

Here is what is included in our Legacy File:

Personal Information
- Debit/Credit Card Copy
- Driver's License Copy
- Pay Stub
- Monthly Budget
- Phone Numbers
- Contact List
- Financial Information
- Bank Account Information
- Email Information

Birth Certificates

Social Security Cards

Passports

Marriage Certificate

Auto Insurance

Homeowner's Insurance

Health Insurance

Life Insurance

Power of Attorney

Wills

Advance Directive for Health Care

Tax Return (Current Year)

Retirement Account Information and Pension Info

Car Titles

Mortgage Information

In addition to having this information at our house, I also made a copy of its contents and put it at my parents' house. This way, if something happened to our file, we have a back-up that we can easily get our hands on. It took me the good part of a Saturday afternoon to gather all of this information, but a few hours is a small price to pay to have all of this in one place for the rest of our lives.

HOMEWORK

Join a professional organization for some protection.

Gather your important documents and create your Legacy File.

CHAPTER 11

Speed up Your Time in The School of Financial Freedom

"In skating over thin ice our safety is in our speed."
RALPH WALDO EMERSON

Now that you know exactly what to do to achieve financial freedom, I'm sure you are excited to make it to 12th grade as quickly as possible. In fact, imagining what it will be like to live a prosperous life and do whatever you want probably has you wishing there was a way you could speed up the amount of time it will take to get there. Well, have I got some GREAT news for you! Here are five great ways to get through the School of Financial Freedom more quickly.

Five Ways to Speed up the Time You Spend in the School of Financial Freedom

1. Reduce Interest Rates on Debt

Unfortunately, once you get into debt, it can be really

difficult to get out. This is because some of your payment is not touching the principal at all; it is only going towards interest. If you have a credit card with a high interest rate, look into transferring it to a 0 percent interest one. This is called a 0 percent balance transfer card. Is your mortgage rate too high? Visit www.bankrate.com to see a list of 0 percent APR credit cards along with current mortgage rates. Spending a few hours lowering the amount you are paying in interest can greatly speed up your time in the School of Financial Freedom!

2. Tax Refund

I know there are some who think it is a bad idea to get a tax refund because you are basically loaning money to the government interest-free. While there is some truth to this, I would much rather get a refund than owe the government more; I have been in both of these situations. You can even view your tax refund as a form of disciplined savings. In addition, if you use your refund to pay off debt, the interest you "earn" by eliminating this debt will far outpace any interest this money would have earned in a bank account.

3. Found Money From Better Budgeting

In a bit, we are going to go over some specific ways you can save money. As you plan your spending each month, you will identify expenses that can be reduced or eliminated. You can use this money to speed up your time spent in the School of Financial Freedom.

4. Sell Some Stuff

Many of us fill all of our available space with stuff. I remember Tracy and I started our married lives in a two-bedroom apartment. After two years, it was full. We then moved to a two-bedroom house that was more than double the size of that apartment. In a couple of years, it was full. We now live in a larger house, and you guessed it, it is full! We have a house for our cars (a garage) that we can't park in sometimes because we have stuff in it. I know some people who have so much stuff they need a storage unit in addition to a house! You might be experiencing the same thing. If you feel you just have too much stuff, have a garage sale or sell it on Ebay and use the proceeds to advance through The School of Financial Freedom.

5. Work an Extra Job/Overtime

I am not saying to do this forever, but acquiring more income can help you get to 12th grade in The School of Financial Freedom much sooner. As a teacher, I have worked both summer school and in the after-school program to earn a little more. While there were some days I was extremely tired, this extra income really helped us. As an added bonus, you are not spending money when you are working! I know some may not have the opportunity to work overtime at their school. If this is the case, you might want to consider working a second job. If you are passionate about a specific product or hobby, you may even consider starting a side business. You never know where this passion could lead you. For example, I had a passion for personal finance and wrote books to help others with their finances. I didn't make a lot from this but every little bit helped. My books also led me to numerous jobs that helped increase my income!

Ways to Save Money (so you can eliminate debt faster)

There are two basic ways to make more money: either increase your income or cut back what you are spending money on. I listed some ways to increase your income above. In Chapter 3 we addressed the importance of the budget and tracking your spending. The reason that tracking your spending is so important is that it makes your plan personal. I can give general money saving tips, but not all of you visit your favorite barista on a daily basis or eat dinner out numerous times a week. Tracking your unique spending habits helps you see exactly how **you** are spending money. However, there are some common ways that we can save money. Here are some of them:

Stop Paying Credit Card Interest

The only thing worse than buying something you can't afford is buying something you don't have the money for and end up paying interest for it. Let's say you decide to upgrade your living room and buy a new television set, couch, and recliner. The total cost is $5,000 and you purchase these items on a credit card with an 18.9 percent interest rate. The minimum payment is 2 percent of the balance which would start at $100/month. If you continued to just make this minimum monthly payment, it would take you over 30 years to pay off, and you would have spent over $19,000 doing so. This is almost four times the purchase price!

Switch Cell Phone Plans

Tracy and I both went a long time without smartphones. When we finally upgraded into the 21st Century, we decided to be as smart (pun intended) about this as possible. Instead of locking into a two-year plan, we both bought used Iphones and signed up for Wal-Mart's Straight Talk plan. We pay a total of $90 a month for both of our phones and have the same service that friends of ours have. Yet some of them pay in excess of $200.

One of my employers paid for my cell phone. After leaving the company, I took over the payment. I stayed with the same carrier to make the transition easier, but for pretty much the same plan I had had with Straight Talk, I was paying over $100 a month! This was more than double what I had been paying before so I quickly switched back to Straight Talk; but, to add a little more insult to injury, I had to pay a $175 cancellation fee. Lesson learned!

Ten years ago many of us did not even have cell phones and got along just fine. Now some pay over $200 a month for their phone plans. If you are looking to cut costs, this may be an area where that you can save some serious cash.

Stop Paying Full Price at the Grocery Store

Tracy really got serious about using coupons in 2010 and the results have been great; since then we have saved over $7,000 by using coupons and shopping for deals. She does not go overboard, and we will never have our own reality show about couponing, but it just shows that shopping smart can help stretch your paycheck. Here are some tips to help you save at the grocery store:

Leave the Spender At Home
In most relationships, there is a spender and saver. The spender seems to be able to spend money on items the saver has never even thought about. You can send the spender to the grocery with a specific list and they still come home with much more. Don't set yourself up for failure: let the spender stay home.

Shop With a List
It's called impulse buying for a reason. We have a tough time resisting the temptation to purchase extras when

shopping. Without a list you will buy items that you simply do not need. Grocery stores are masterful at placing tempting items at the ends of aisles to get your attention. Even worse is when you forget to purchase the actual item you went to the store for in the first place. If you are cooking at home, pre-plan a rough menu and make a list before going grocery shopping. Getting all the food you need in one trip can help you avoid another unnecessary trip and the temptations that go along with that.

Shop the Sales

In addition to using coupons, you can also shop sales. Most grocery stores have sales cycles in which certain items go on sale every few weeks. Take some time to note this and plan your spending in advance. Do this and you will never pay full price again!

Don't Shop Hungry

Going to the store after a long day of work is self-sabotage. When you are tired and hungry you will be tempted to buy the first thing that smells good. Tracy usually goes shopping on a non-workday morning after eating breakfast. As an added bonus, the store is less crowded!

Leave the Kids at Home

If you have children, this tip is pretty obvious. When Tracy brings Ava or Ella with her, she **always** spends more. Let the kids stay home with the spender and it will be much easier to stick with the list.

When Eating out, Stop Splurging on Appetizers and Drinks

The portions at restaurants seem to increase as fast as

our country's average waist size. If you are like me, you usually need a to-go box because you cannot eat your entire meal. Why pay more money for an appetizer when all it does is take up space in your belly before your meal is even brought out? In addition, soft drinks and sweet tea can now cost over $2. If you have a family of four, that is over $8 for drinks alone. Order water instead, and you can save lots of money. I have a friend who used to pay his children a dollar if they ordered water instead of a soda. He taught them a lesson and saved money at the same time.

Stop Paying Overdraft Fees

There is truly no excuse for this. If you balance your checkbook and spend less than you earn, you will never have to spend any of your hard-earned money on these expensive fees.

Stop Signing up for Quick Delivery

In the instant gratification days we live in, many people order things online and have these items shipped by priority mail. If you cannot wait the standard shipping time frame (usually between 5-10 days) for something to arrive, you may want to consider doing without that item completely.

Don't Buy Designer Kid's and Baby's Clothes

Until your child stops growing inches every year, there is no need to buy the newest fashion clothes for him. Why waste $25 on a shirt he will wear two or three times? This is especially true when it comes to dressing our babies. Why spend a lot of money on something that only gets spit up on?

Rethink Your Gym Membership

I am all for exercising, but many people who have gym memberships haven't been there in six months. It is very easy to buy into the hype and set a New Year's resolution to lose weight and join a gym. Unfortunately, after enthusiasm wanes around Valentine's Day, the monthly dues do not stop coming out of your bank account. If you want to get in shape, you can do many healthy things for little cost. I have run nine half-marathons in the past six years, and the only thing it cost me was the price of good running shoes.

Ditch Your Satellite Television and
Premium Cable Packages

Don't get me wrong, I enjoy watching television, especially sports. I even order the NFL package so I can watch my beloved Miami Dolphins every fall Sunday. However, some of us have over 200 channels and only watch a few of them. If you are looking for ways to save some serious money, this might be a good place to start. Sure, you may not be able to keep up with those "real" housewives, but since a few of them have filed for bankruptcy, who would want to anyway?

Stop Having Car Payments

According to Experian Automotive, the average monthly payment on a new vehicle is $483. The average used-car payment was $361.[a] As you can easily see, driving a used car can save you some serious money; even better, drive a car as long as possible. I drive a 2002 car and have not had a car payment on it since 2004!

Quit Buying Name-Brand Paper Products

Think about it: you use paper towels, napkins, and plates only once (even I don't re-use these!). Spending more for the name-brand version of these products is a big waste. Buy the generic brand instead and save.

Start Drinking Regular Coffee Instead of Using K-Cups

I know many people now use Keurigs or a similar type of machine to brew coffee. For convenience, many use k-cups. Instead, purchase the filters for these machines and buy regular coffee. Yes, you have to clean these out, but the time is definitely worth the cost. I priced the cost of k-cups compared to ground coffee and was very surprised at how much more you will pay when buying individual pods. This was the same exact brand and style of coffee. You would pay $2.02 per ounce for the k-cups compared with $0.07 an ounce for the ground coffee. That is a savings of $1.95 per ounce!

Brown Bag Your Lunch

I know it can be a challenge to plan ahead and pack your lunch, but it can save you a lot of money. Let's say you eat lunch out every day during the work week. We will keep it cheap and say you eat fast food and spend only $5 per meal. Most of us won't miss that $5 or even think twice about spending it. Well, $5 per day Monday to Friday equals $25 a week, $100 a month and $1,300 a year. That's a lot of money!

Avoid the Box Office

I realize going out to the movies can be a fun way to

spend an evening, but it is definitely costly. If you are going to the movie theater twice each month, you are spending a lot of money in exchange for a few hours of entertainment. We are not even including the snacks because who can go to the movies and resist the $8 bucket of popcorn and $5 soda? Wait a few months until the movie comes out at Redbox and pop your own popcorn at home. You get to watch the same film and eat the same food at a greatly reduced price.

Get New Home and Auto Insurance Quotes

This is often an overlooked expense that can result in huge savings! I know from first-hand experience how much this can save you. I recently got new quotes on my insurance. I had not even thought about this since we moved to Georgia years ago. I met with a local insurance agent for one hour and saved over $1,200/year on my homeowner's insurance and almost $300/year on my car insurance! Get new quotes on these every two years.

Iron Your Own Clothes

This may not work for everyone, but ironing your own clothes instead of using a dry cleaner can save you some money. I can honestly say I have never had anything dry cleaned. It does take me some time to iron my shirts but I usually just let them pile. When there is a game on, I iron while I watch it.

Save on Sporting Events

Sporting events can be an expensive venture. I do not go to live games often, but every year for Mother's Day, I brave the Atlanta traffic and take my mom to watch the

Dodgers play the Braves (she is a huge L.A. Dodger fan). I use the website www.scorebig.com and save on the price of our tickets. They offer up to 60 percent savings on certain tickets. This helps lessen the blow of spending $6 on a hot dog.

Don't Buy Expensive Razors

Another convenient way to save is to purchase razors from www.dollarshaveclub.com. I signed up for their Humble Twin Razor and receive five cartridges every month for just $3. The cartridges I used before cost me $2.25 each. If you do not shave much, you can even adjust how often you receive refills and have them delivered every other month.

Kids Eat Free

You can save serious money by choosing to eat at home, but sometimes we choose to give ourselves (or, in my case, my wife) a break from cooking. If you have children and are planning to eat out, check out www.outtoeatwithkids.com. This site lists restaurants near you where kids eat free or at a reduced cost.

Dollar Store Shopping

Many of us have great intentions when shopping at this type of store, but end up walking out with a bunch of junk we really should not have bought. Despite that, you can really save when purchasing certain items from these stores, including cleaning supplies, birthday cards, coloring books, wrapping paper, and party supplies. Just remember to stick with your list and don't let those shiny objects jump into your cart.

Drink Tap Water

A final way to save is to drink tap water. According to a report, Americans drink an average of 270 bottles of water each year.[b] If the price of a bottle of water was $1.00, a family of four would spend over $1,000 a year—on water!

I know, all work and no play makes Jack a dull boy. I completely get it and am not saying you have to utilize every cost-cutting item. But applying some of them can lead to some serious savings which can help you achieve financial freedom faster.

Most of us can't have it all. If you don't want to cancel your satellite or cable package, that is fine. However, cut back in another area. Every financial action has a financial consequence. The lack of thinking about the consequences is what gets so many into financial trouble. If I make $50,000 a year, there is no way I can truly afford a $300,000 house. I don't care how much I qualify for: I cannot afford it!

I will never forget explaining this concept to Ava. Before attending elementary school, Ava mostly stayed home and Tracy watched her. She did go to a friend's house occasionally, but Tracy and I were friends with these children's parents and most of them lived like we did and did not buy a lot of toys for their children, because the budget didn't allow it. Elementary school opened Ava's eyes to how others lived. One day after entering kindergarten, she came home with a great question. We were in her room and she asked, "Dad, can we move to a bigger house? Most of the kids in my class talk about how big their houses are and some even have extra rooms to put all their toys in." What a great teaching moment! I told her we could absolutely move but a few things would change. First, Ava liked having Tracy waiting at home for her every day after school. Well, that would have to change because Tracy would have to get a job so that we could afford a bigger house. Ava also loved having her daddy teach at the same school she attended (I did too!). If we moved to a bigger house, that would change, too, because I would have to get a higher-paying job and leave teaching. Finally, even though she would have a bigger house and possibly more toys to play with, Ava would not be home as much because Tracy and I would have to work longer. She would be put in the after-school program, and we would pick her up after 5:00 most days. After explaining these consequences to her, Ava replied, "Dad, I think we have it pretty good."

Sure, there are times I wish I had nicer stuff. Like most people, if I see someone pull up next to me in a shiny new BMW, of course I want it! I can have it, but something would have to change because of that decision. Since the day I married Tracy, I have not seen one object that made me want to change the way we are living. This all comes back to Kindergarten in The School of Financial Freedom. We have goals in place we are working towards. Accomplishing these goals means much more than any shiny piece of metal ever will.

Specific Ways Teachers Can Supplement Their Salary

We mentioned some general ways for you to earn and save more money. Here are some specific ways that teachers can increase their income:

Teach Overseas

I wrote about how wonderful an experience this was for Tracy and me. We grew so much as a couple; there's nothing like being able to speak only to your spouse for the majority of the time through two years to strengthen a marriage. In addition, it gave us a great start to our financial futures. I mentioned we used a company named International Schools Services. If this is something that interests you, please visit their website at www.iss.edu.

Tutoring

As an educator, you are an expert in your field. Because this is the case, some will be willing to pay you to help their child improve in school. When I taught first grade, one of my student's parents asked me to tutor their son. They were willing to pay me $50 an hour to do so. Since this was "extra" money and not needed for our expenses, I decided to just throw this money into a jar and forget about it. About nine months later, Tracy told me we were going on a surprise trip the following month to celebrate my 30th birthday (she didn't tell me where we were going). By the time the trip came, I had over $1,000 saved! We ended up going to New York City for the first time and my tutoring money paid for some of the hotel and all of our spending money! Now, putting this money into a jar was not the smartest financial move because it didn't earn any interest but because I knew this money was going to be spent soon, I decided to just keep accumulating it at home.

Working in the After School Program

Most schools have an after-school program and are usually desperate for help. I know this might be the last thing you want to do after spending all day teaching, but it is a good way to add a little to your monthly check. You don't have to do it every day in most cases, you can even pick and choose which days.

When I taught a special needs class, one of my students stayed after school. Since he had a severe mental disability, he required one-on-one support. I decided to take this on a couple of days each week. This helped us greatly when Tracy was not working. I always picked Friday and another day of the week. It is amazing how many were ready to start the weekend as early as possible. I thought Fridays were great because I knew I had the weekend coming up after staying at school until 6:00. One great thing about working the after school program is that you are already there so you don't need to drive anywhere!

Teaching Homebound

This might not apply to all, but there are some students that are too sick and/or fragile to come to school. They are placed on Homebound services in which a teacher comes to their house to teach them a few hours a week.
I had one such student in my class and did this for two years. Every Monday and Thursday I would leave school once my students were gone and drive to his house and teach him for an hour and a half. I got paid my hourly rate along with mileage. Similar to the money I earned from tutoring years ago, I just put this "extra" money in a jar (don't come looking around my house for this: I now put any extra money we have in the bank ☺) and let it accumulate.

After doing this for over a year, Tracy and I decided to do something that we had wanted to for a long time with Ava and Ella, but hadn't been able to justify taking the cost from my salary. So, one Saturday morning we got into the car and drove to Florida. We told the girls we were going to stay at their cousins' house for a few days over the Thanksgiving Break. The next morning we told them we had an errand to run and asked them to come with us. We then drove to DISNEY WORLD and spent a magical three days there! We did not spend a dime out of our monthly pay; this trip was solely paid for with money I earned by teaching homebound students.

In addition to these opportunities, many of you have summers off (I know summer is becoming shorter and shorter). If you needed to bring in a little income you could take a summer job and basically earn two checks during this time, as you are still getting paid your teaching salary. Many summer camps would love to have a teacher as a camp counselor so this could be a possibility for you to increase your income a bit.

HOMEWORK

What is one action you can take right now to save money and speed up the time it will take for you to achieve financial freedom?

CONCLUSION

"Take the first step in faith. You don't have to see the whole staircase, just take the first step."
MARTIN LUTHER KING, JR.

Think back to when you were younger and what your plans, hopes, and dreams were. Many of us had some great ideas of what our lives would be like when were adults. I was either going to be the next Dale Murphy and hit home runs out of Fulton County Stadium, or Dan Marino and march my beloved Miami Dolphins up and down Joe Robbie Stadium.

Unfortunately, something happens when we hit adulthood. We no longer dream big. Now obviously I wasn't Major League Baseball or NFL material, but we still need to have some dreams, albeit more realistic ones. However, many of us settle for less. Sometimes we even fool ourselves and think, "Once I ... , I will be happy." Fill in the blank with "make more money," "marry that perfect person," "buy that nice car," etc. Once we achieve this status, we are happy for a moment, but then it is on to the next item. In essence, we set ourselves up for disappointment. I think it is important to dream big, but also to recognize the blessings many of us take for granted. I am reminded of one of my favorite reads about an American Businessman and a Mexican Fisherman.

The Story of the Mexican Fisherman

An American investment banker was at the pier of a small coastal Mexican village when a small boat with just one fisherman docked. Inside the small boat were several large Yellowfin tuna. The American complimented the fisherman on the quality of his fish, and he asked how long it took to catch them.

The fisherman replied, "Only a little while." The American then asked why didn't he stay out longer and catch more fish? The fisherman said that he had enough to support his family's immediate needs. The American then asked, "But what do you do with the rest of your time?"

The Mexican fisherman said, "I sleep late, fish a little, play with my children, take siestas with my wife, Maria, stroll into the village each evening where I sip wine, and play guitar with my amigos. I have a full and busy life." The American scoffed, "I am a Harvard MBA and could help you. You should spend more time fishing, and with the proceeds, buy a bigger boat. With the proceeds from the bigger boat, you could buy several boats; eventually you would have a fleet of fishing boats. Instead of selling your catch to a middleman you would sell directly to the processor, eventually opening your own cannery. You would control the product, processing, and distribution. You would need to leave this small coastal fishing village and move to Mexico City, then LA, and eventually New York City, where you will run your expanding enterprise.

The Mexican fisherman asked, "But, how long will this all take?"

To which the American replied, "15 - 20 years."

"But what then?" asked the fisherman.

The American laughed and said, "That's the best part. When the time is right you would announce an IPO and sell your company stock to the public and become very rich. You would make millions!"

"Millions—then what?"

The American said, "Then you would retire. Move to a small coastal fishing village where you would sleep late, fish a little, play with your kids, take siestas with your wife, stroll to the village in the evenings where you could sip wine, and play your guitar with your amigos."

I bet many of you can relate to that. I love how far we have come with modern technology but sometimes feel it also takes away from us. Most of us know two speeds: fast and faster! Our "Things To Do List" seems to go on and on and once we accomplish one task, it is on to the next item on the list. Establishing goals and going about achieving them are extremely important (that is why they are Kindergarten in The School of Financial Freedom) but far too many of us never stop and take time to reflect on what we have accomplished and been blessed with. I encourage you to try and find some time every day to reflect on your blessings. I promise if you do this, you will realize how "rich" you are.

Finish Strong

A few years ago, Tracy came home and said we needed to challenge ourselves. At the time I was still teaching in a self-contained Severe/Profound classroom so I thought I was being challenged on an almost daily basis, but she did not see it that way. She suggested running a half-marathon. At this point in my life, I had never run more than three miles, so I thought there was no way I would ever be able to run 13.1 miles! Even though this seemed next to impossible, I thought I'd give it a try.

We found a training plan and increased our mileage almost every week. The first week, we were just doing one-mile runs. In twelve weeks, we were up to six miles and, after 18 weeks, we both ran a half-marathon! Since then, I have run a total of nine half-marathons. When training for these races, the most difficult step I take is always the first one. In fact, sometimes the hardest part of my run is lacing up my shoes. But after I do this and take that first step, momentum begins to help me. Once this happens, each subsequent step becomes a little easier. This is true of doing better with your money, too. Whether you are building up that emergency fund, getting out of debt, or saving for retirement, that first step is always the most difficult. Once you get going, it becomes easier and easier. Now, you may run into some tough spots (just like facing that long, steep hill on mile 7) but, because you have had success, you will feel confident that you can push through and keep going. There will probably be some days in which you feel like   giving up. Please don't! Keep taking one step at a time and you will reach all of your financial goals.

Love: Perhaps the Key to Financial Success

In this book, I have focused on giving you the tools and information you need to equip yourself to achieve financial freedom. However, something I have not mentioned yet might be the key to winning with money: LOVE!

In the book of Mark, Jesus discusses how important love is: *And one of the scribes came up and heard them disputing with one another, and seeing that he answered them well, asked him, "Which commandment is the most important of all?" Jesus answered, "The most important is, 'Hear, O Israel: The Lord our God, the Lord is one. And you shall love the Lord your God with all your heart and with all your soul and with all your mind and with all your strength.' The second is this, 'You shall love your neighbor as yourself.' There is no other commandment greater than these.* "[a]

I have always tried to practice this and have realized first-hand how important it is to love others. As I mentioned earlier, I was recently laid-off from my job. After word got out, I had numerous people looking to help me in any way they could. In fact, one of my friends hired me to work at his company for seven weeks until I was able to find another job!

You can make all the correct financial decisions in life and still be poor. I have known others who had a lot of money but no positive relationships. No matter how large their bank accounts were, I would never classify them as being wealthy.

I have spent most of this book discussing the importance of having savings, getting out of debt, investing for retirement and making other sound financial decisions. However, I also think you should work on creating what best-selling author Jon Acuff refers to as a "career savings account." This account consists of relationships, skills, character and hustle.[b] After being laid-off, my career savings account enabled me to get back on track!

The Most Important Things in Life

I know it can be really discouraging to try and get our finances on track. We have lessons plans to do, meals to cook, and events to attend. When it seems like you just don't have enough time in the day to accomplish all that needs to be done, here is a story that shows us what is really important:

A professor stood before his philosophy class and had some items in front of him. When the class began, he wordlessly picked up a very large and empty mayonnaise jar and proceeded to fill it with golf balls. He then asked the students if the jar was full. They agreed that it was. The professor then picked up a box of pebbles and poured them into the jar. He shook the jar lightly. The pebbles rolled into the open areas between the golf balls. He then asked the students again if the jar was full. They agreed it was.

The professor next picked up a box of sand and poured it into the jar. Of course, the sand filled up everything else. He asked once more if the jar was full. The students responded with a unanimous "yes."

The professor then produced two cups of coffee from under the table and poured the entire contents into the jar, effectively filling the empty space between the sand. The students laughed.

"Now," said the professor as the laughter subsided, "I want you to recognize that this jar represents your life. The golf balls are the important things— your family, your children, your health, your friends, and your favorite passions— and if everything else was lost and only they remained, your life would still be full. The pebbles are the other things that matter like your job, your house, and your car. The sand is everything else: the small stuff. "If you put the sand into the jar first," he continued, "there is no room for the pebbles or the golf balls. The same goes for life. If you spend all your time and energy on the small stuff you will never have room for the things that are important to you. "Pay attention to the things that are critical to your happiness. Play with your children. Take time to get medical checkups. Take your spouse out to dinner. Play another 18. There will always be time to clean the house and fix the disposal. Take care of the golf balls first: the things that really matter. Set your priorities. The rest is just sand."

One of the students raised her hand and inquired what the coffee represented.

The professor smiled. "I'm glad you asked. It just goes to show you that no matter how full your life may seem, there's always room for a couple of cups of coffee with a friend."

While you are focusing on gaining control of your finances, I hope you will remember to fill your jar with the important stuff!

Thank you so much for choosing to become an educator and making this world a better place. Good luck on this journey and God bless!

Financial Education Is a Journey

My number one goal in writing this book was to show you first-hand that you can manage your money well on a teacher's salary. However, like you all know, one teacher alone cannot cover everything. After reading this book, I hope you are excited to learn and grow even more. Below are a list of books that have helped me greatly on my own financial and life journey.

For Financial Growth

The Automatic Millionaire: A Powerful One-Step Plan to Live and Finish Rich, by David Bach

The Richest Man in Babylon, by George Clason

Rich Habits - The Daily Success Habits of Wealthy Individuals, by Thomas C. Corley

You Can Retire Sooner Than You Think, by Wes Moss

The Total Money Makeover: Classic Edition: A Proven Plan for Financial Fitness, by Dave Ramsey

Your Money or Your Life: 9 Steps to Transforming Your Relationship with Money and Achieving Financial Independence, by Vicki Robin and Joe Dominguez

I Was Broke. Now I'm Not. by Joseph Sangl

The Millionaire Next Door: The Surprising Secrets of America's Wealthy, by Thomas J. Stanley and William D. Danko

For Personal Growth

Start: Punch Fear in the Face, Escape Average and Do Work that Matters, by Jon Acuff

The Traveler's Gift: Seven Decisions that Determine Personal Success, by Andy Andrews

The Alchemist, by Paulo Coelho

One Question: Life-Changing Answers from Today's Leading Voices, by Ken Coleman

The 7 Habits of Highly Effective People: Powerful Lessons in Personal Change, by Stephen R. Covey

48 Days to the Work You Love: Preparing for the New Normal, by Dan Miller and Dave Ramsey

Start with Why: How Great Leaders Inspire Everyone to Take Action, by Simon Sinek

ACKNOWLEDGEMENTS

Thank you God for giving me the gifts to help others handle their money better. I hope to continue using Your blessings to make this world a better place.

Tracy, thank you so much for being the best wife and the best mommy to Ava and Ella. You use your gifts daily to make others have a better life and are the best person I know. You are my personal cheerleader. I am blessed to spend my life with you.

Ava and Ella, thank you for being my daughters. I love being your daddy every single day and think both of you are amazing young ladies.

Mom, Dad, Meno and Art, thank you for the path you have set for me. Your examples of what being truly wealthy looks like continue to inspire and guide me.

Nancy—WOW—another book! Thank you for your unconditional support. I remember after my first book you told me that I was like family. You are so much more than my publisher and I am eternally grateful to you for allowing me to spread my message.

Finally, to all you teachers out there: you could have picked a much easier profession and made a lot more money, but you chose to make a difference. Thank you for all of your dedication and love.

Danny is currently a special education teacher in Georgia. He has also taught pre-k, kindergarten, first grade, second grade and sixth grade.

In addition to this book, Danny is the author of three other personal finance books: *A Bright Financial Future: Teaching Kids About Money Pre-K through College for Life-Long Success; A Simple Book of Financial Wisdom: Teach Yourself (and Your Kids) How to Live Wealthy with Little Money;* and *How To Survive (and perhaps thrive) On A Teacher's Salary.* When Danny's daughter, Ava, was nine years old, she also traditionally published her very own money book for kids, *The Financial Angel: What All Kids Should Know About Money (Ages 4-11).*

Danny's everyday approach to handling money has led him to be interviewed on   numerous television shows, including *Fox & Friends, The CBS Early Show, CNN's Newsroom, Fox News Channel's Happening Now, The 700 Club, The Clark Howard Show,* and *MSNBC Live.* He has also been interviewed on over 600 radio shows and featured in numerous publications such as *USA Today, Instructor Magazine, Woman's Day, Yahoo.com, The Wall Street Journal, Consumer Reports, Money Magazine,* and *The Atlanta Journal Constitution.* Danny wants to show other school teachers how to thrive on their salaries too.

Learn more:

www.wealthyteacher.weebly.com

ADDED BONUS!

Visit my website and fill in the contact form—tell me where you bought, borrowed, or found this book, and I will send you a free pdf: *How to Save $30,000 this Year.*

NOTES

Chapter 1

a. http://www.bankrate.com/banking/savings/financial-security-0617/

b. http://www1.cbn.com/guard-against-greed

c. http://www.businessinsider.com/openfolio-teachers-are-good-investors-2015-3

d. http://www.redcrowmarketing.com/2015/09/10/many-ads-see-one-day/

e. http://www.investopedia.com/articles/financialcareers/10/buffett-frugal.asp

f. http://blogs.wsj.com/bankruptcy/2015/08/04/50-cent-bankruptcy-by-the-numbers/

g. http://www.bankrate.com/finance/celebrity-money/musicians-bankruptcy-marvin-gaye.aspx

h. http://usatoday30.usatoday.com/life/people/2004-04-26-don-johnson_x.htm

i. http://www.moneycrashers.com/bankrupt-celebrities-rich-broke/

j. http://richhabits.net/dave-ramsey-rich-habits-tom-corley/#more-365

Chapter 2

a. http://www.nydailynews.com/life-style/majority-u-s-workers-not-engaged-job-gallup-poll-article-1.2094990

b. http://www.huffingtonpost.com/2015/05/04/public-school-teachers-underpaid_n_7201794.html

c. http://blogs.edweek.org/teachers/teaching_now/2014/07/ teacher-salary-growth-weak-in-the-united-states.html

d. http://content.time.com/time/magazine/article/0,9171,2019628,00.
html

e. http://www.businessinsider.com/most-meaningful-jobs-in-amer-
ica-2015-7

Chapter 3

a. http://www.investopedia.com/articles/pf/08/pay-in-cash.asp

b. http://www.jstor.org/stable/10.1086/661730?seq=1#page_scan_tab_
contents

c. https://www.institutedfa.com/Leading-Causes-Divorce/

d. http://www.forbes.com/sites/jennagoudreau/2011/01/13/is-your-
partner-cheating-on-you-financially-31-admit-money-deception-infi
delity-red-flags-money-lies/

e. https://medium.com/@agmsnodgrass/8-ways-to-get-on-the-same-
page-about-money-with-your-spouse-1f9382b36143

f. http://www.myfinancialawareness.com/Topics%20Financial/
Myth%20-%20Money%20is%20the%20Number%20One%20Cause
%20of%20Divorce.htm

Chapter 4

a. http://www.theatlantic.com/magazine/archive/2016/05/my-secret-
shame/476415/

b. http://www.daveramsey.com/articles/print/articleID/four-must-
have-insurance-policies/

c. https://en.wikipedia.org/wiki/Terri_Schiavo_case

d. http://www.foxbusiness.com/features/2014/09/05/how-much-
youre-losing-by-not-getting-your-employer-401k-match.html

e. https://www.bls.gov/news.release/hsgec.nr0.htm

f. http://www.usatoday.com/story/money/personalfinance/
2015/03/17/paying-tuition-outweighs-saving-for-retirement/70152912/

g.http://www.collegedata.com/cs/content/content_payarticle_tmpl.jht ml?articleId=10064

h. https://www.finra.org/newsroom/2016/study-finds-1-3-student-loan-holders-payments-due-are-late-payments-and-more-half

Chapter 6

a. http://blogs.wsj.com/economics/2015/05/08/congratulations-class-of-2015-youre-the-most-indebted-ever-for-now/

b. http://www.costofwedding.com

c. http://www.usgovernmentdebt.us

d. http://www.cnn.com/2009/LIVING/02/04/trillion.dollars/

e. https://www.facebook.com/notes/dan-asmussen/what-a-trillion-dollars-looks-like-a-visualization-of-us-debt/10150303103185432

f. http://www.creditcards.com/credit-card-news/credit-card-vending-machines-increase-sales-1273.php#ixzz46DmkOHsH

g. https://www.nerdwallet.com/blog/credit-cards/credit-cards-make-you-spend-more/

Chapter 8

a. http://www.politifact.com/texas/statements/2015/apr/09/ bernie-s/bernie-sanders-says-half-americans-have-less-10000/

b. http://fortune.com/2015/04/21/retirement-savings-survey/

c. https://personal.vanguard.com/us/insights/retirement/plan-for-a-long-retirement-tool

d. http://www.npr.org/news/specials/enron/

e. https://finance.yahoo.com/quote/brk-a?ltr=1

f. http://www.daveramsey.com/blog/how-to-minimize-risk-in-shaky-market

g. http://tradingninvestment.com/stock-market-historical-returns/

h. https://www.cnbc.com/2017/06/18/the-sp-500-has-already-met-its-average-return-for-a-full-year.html

i. http://www.usatoday.com/story/money/cars/2015/05/04/new-car-transaction-price-3-kbb-kelley-blue-book/26690191/

Chapter 9

a. http://www.bls.gov/news.release/cesan.nr0.htm

b. http://www.freeby50.com/2012/12/what-percent-of-tax-filers-itemize.html

c. http://syndication.nationaljournal.com/communications/Allstate%20National%20Journal%20Heartland%20Monitor%20TOPLINE%20FINAL.pdf

Chapter 10

a. http://nypost.com/2014/07/13/four-city-teachers-rake-in-millions-while-banned-from-classrooms/

Chapter 11

a. https://www.edmunds.com/car-news/average-monthly-car-payment-pegged-at-483-study-says.html

b. https://www.washingtonpost.com/news/wonk/wp/2015/08/28/americas-growing-love-affair-with-the-most-wasteful-thing-to-drink-there-is/

Conclusion

a. https://www.biblegateway.com/passage/?search=Mark+12%3A28-31&version=ESV

b. https://www.cnbc.com/2017/01/23/bestselling-author-explains-why-to-invest-in-a-career-savings-account.html

CPSIA information can be obtained
at www.ICGtesting.com
Printed in the USA
BVOW08s0332170118
505324BV00001B/71/P